From Shack to White House: A Memoir of Four Lives

Theo W. Braddy

Published by RoeWrites4U, 2025.

While every precaution has been taken in the preparation of this book, the publisher assumes no responsibility for errors or omissions, or for damages resulting from the use of the information contained herein.

FROM SHACK TO WHITE HOUSE: A MEMOIR OF FOUR LIVES

First edition. December 7, 2025.

Copyright © 2025 Theo W. Braddy.

ISBN: 979-8993899213

Written by Theo W. Braddy.

Table of Contents

Foreword 1
Table of Contents 4
Prologue 5
Part I – My First Life: The Able-Bodied Experience 7
Chapter 1: Grandma's Cookies 8
Chapter 2: Dad's Dimes 10
Chapter 3: A Night I'll Never Forget 11
Chapter 4: Brother Gone, Brother Returned 12
Chapter 5: Losing My Brother 13
Chapter 6: The Knife Fight 14
Chapter 7: The Tire Jack Incident 15
Chapter 8: The Candy Caper 16
Chapter 9: The Mud Hole 17
Chapter 10: First Heartbreak 19
Chapter 11: The Internship – My first glimpse of disability 20
Chapter 12: The Coach's Favorite 22
Chapter 13: Game Night Glory 23
Chapter 14: She Picked Me 24
Part II – My Second Life: The Disabled Experience 25
Chapter 1: The Day It Happened 26
Chapter 2: The Ambulance Rides 28
Chapter 3: The Screws That Caused Pain, Relieved Pain 29
Chapter 4: A Visit from Coach 31
Chapter 5: My New Home: Doctor's Hospital 32
Chapter 6: Warm Springs 34
Chapter 7: Going Home: Shack, Faith and Healing 37
Chapter 8: Back to School 39
Chapter 9: The Nursing Home Experience 41
Chapter 10: My Family Saved Me 43
Chapter 11: Elizabethtown Hospital for Crippled Children 45
Chapter 12: The Island of Misfits 48

The Game Changer 51
The Great Equalizer 52
Chapter 13: Early One Morning..................................... 53
Chapter 14: Edinboro University – What Was I Thinking? 56
Chapter 15: Temple University — My MSW 60
The Cold Night.. 62
Chapter 16: My Tribe 64
Chapter 17: "Mr. Braddy, You Just Won a Championship: What's Next?".. 66
Part III – My Third Life: The Leader Within: Family & Community Leadership 68
Chapter 1: A Few Thoughts on Family Leadership 69
Chapter 2: Iron Sharpens Iron 70
Chapter 3: You Can't Do That! 71
Chapter 4: I Can't See It, but I have Faith 74
Chapter 5: My Experiences as Coach 75
Chapter 6: Can I Have Fries with that? 77
Chapter 7: The Unexpected Guest 80
Chapter 8: There He Goes... 81
Chapter 9: Woody's.. 84
Chapter 10: The Great Escape 86
Chapter 11: There's No Place Like Home 88
Chapter 12: A Few Thoughts on Community Leadership........... 92
Chapter 13: Live Well Fitness Center 93
Chapter 14: Community Leader..................................... 95
Chapter 15: Here's the Keys 96
Chapter 16: Justin Dart — "Lead On. I Love You!" 100
Chapter 17: Maggie Shreve — The Architect of Independent Living Standards 102
Chapter 18: Christina Forbrich — The Standard of Excellence 103
Chapter 19: The Late Mayor Stephen Reed — From Adversary to Ally... 104

Chapter 20: The First Marriage 105
Chapter 21: The Breaking Point 107
Chapter 22: The Immoveable Force 110
Chapter 23: The Second Marriage 115
Chapter 24: Well-Intentional Folks 117
Chapter 25: Out of the Blue 119
Part IV – My Fourth Life: Legacy and Impact 121
Chapter 1: A Few Thoughts on Legacy and Impact 122
Chapter 2: Riding Off into the Sunset 123
Chapter 3: From Token to Trailblazer 126
Chapter 4: The Great Senator Bob Casey 129
Chapter 5: The Perfect Fit 132
The Call. 138
Chapter 6: Meeting the Moment - Anna 143
Chapter 7: We Can't Go Back - Alison 150
Chapter 8: Vice President Harris 153
Chapter 9: President Biden 156
Part V: Bonus Hits - Lessons Along the Way 158
Redefining Success 159
The Power of "You Said" 160
Two Ears, One Mouth 161
Pick Your Battles 162
Words That Matter 163
Challenges and Failure 164
Making God Smile 165
Recognition vs. Impact 166
Living Well 167
Be a Guide. 168
Remember the Mission 169
Epilogue 170
Memoir Glossary 172
Endorsement 175

THEO W. BRADDY

From Shack to White House

A MEMOIR OF FOUR LIVES

From Shack to White House: A Memoir of Four Lives
© 2025 by Theo W. Braddy
All rights reserved. No part of this publication may be reproduced, stored in a retrieval system, or transmitted in any form or by any means—electronic, mechanical, photocopying, recording, or otherwise—without the prior written permission of the author, except for brief quotations used in reviews or critical articles.
Published by RoeWrites4U
Camphill, PA
ISBN: 979-8-9938992-1-3
Cover design by Ira Postoronka
Edited by RoeWrites4U

First Edition
For more information, visit: RoeWrites4U.com

Foreword

From the first time I met Theo, I knew we would do something important together. I was leading the Administration for Community Living, and he had just become the Executive Director of the National Council on Independent Living. The disability community was reeling from the devastating impact of the COVID-19 pandemic. We were doing everything we could in our respective roles to address the immediate and urgent needs of disabled people. But we both understood that while our response was necessary, it was not enough. What we really needed was to take on the long-standing, systemic discrimination and barriers that had become visible during – but were not unique to – the pandemic.

We immediately formed a deep connection. Theo is the perfect combination of big ideas and principles, along with a get-it-done attitude. We found in each other a partner ready to seize an opportunity to make the world a more just, inclusive place. And we had quite the opportunity before us!

I was helping lead an update to the "Section 504 rules" for the first time since the historic "504 sit-ins" almost 50 years ago, and Theo quickly became an invaluable collaborator. Section 504 of the Rehabilitation Act is the foundation of disability rights. The law prohibits disability discrimination in all programs and activities that receive federal funding, reaching hospitals, doctors' offices, and states' Medicaid and disability service systems. The pandemic had shone a spotlight on the long-standing discrimination that disabled people endure in the health care system – from denials of lifesaving treatment to inaccessible medical equipment and segregation in institutions – and created the momentum and urgency to update the rules.

After more than two years of hard work in an unprecedented partnership between the federal government and the disability community, we released updated rules that are the strongest tool we've ever had to address the health disparities and discrimination that too many disabled people face every day. Theo and I both view the Section 504 rules as one of the most important disability policies in decades.

Working closely with Theo, I learned who he was as a person and leader. I saw how his own experiences with discrimination – some of the very types we were working to prohibit in these new rules – fueled his determination. Theo exemplifies a quality that I often say is one of the greatest strengths of the disability community: grit. Grit is the combination of focus and perseverance. It's an unwavering focus on a clear long-term goal and the ferocious determination to work hard to reach it. Grit is finding a way around every roadblock and getting back up when you get knocked down. It's a combination of passion and resiliency. As you read Theo's memoir, you will see he truly embodies our community's grit.

I also learned about leadership from Theo. He is the definition of a servant leader, always listening to, centering, and empowering the people who are most impacted. He prioritizes the needs of the community and measures success by his impact on the lives of others. Theo is a man of deep faith, and it is clear that his motivation to serve comes from a higher force.

As we were planning the event to announce the final Section 504 rules, I knew Theo had to be the one to speak about their importance. For anyone who has heard Theo speak, he is the quintessential preacher, powerfully weaving together personal, moral, and legal aspects into one.

There are some speeches that stand the test of time. Theo's speech that day will be one of those. Everyone in the room got chills, hearing him speak about how together we had punched ableism in the face and his hope that it would be a knock-out punch. He warned us, however, that it would be up to us to fight for it. I think of Theo's call-to-action almost daily now, as we are fighting unprecedented rollbacks in disability rights and the critical services that make those rights a reality.

His words have never rung more true. (I encourage you to listen to his speech, which starts around minute 17, visit here: https://www.youtube.com/watch?v=mYliKkvNi98).

I am privileged to call Theo a colleague and friend. I have deep gratitude for his courage and honesty in sharing his powerful disability journey with all of us. It is not the usual disability story that is told. Theo's memoir brings an important perspective to the disability narrative. Reading his memoir added fuel to my motivation to fight for a world where every person is valued and included, particularly in these challenging and uncertain times. I believe it will have the same impact on you.

— Alison Barkoff
https://www.linkedin.com/in/alison-barkoff-31b363135

From Shack to White House: A Memoir of Four Lives
By Theo W. Braddy

Prologue

People often ask, "How did you cope with becoming disabled at fifteen?"

My answer is always the same: I started a new life and closed the chapter on the old one.

I haven't lived just one life, I've lived four. Each one distinct, each one carrying its own lessons, heartbreaks, and triumphs.

The first began in a little shack with a tin roof and no inside plumbing.

The second began on a football field, the day I became paralyzed.

The third began when I discovered my voice as a leader.

And the fourth, well, that one began in the White House.

Each one distinct, each one carrying its own lessons, heartbreaks, and triumphs.

And yes, there was loss, but each life taught me how to start again.

This memoir is organized by those four lives, each a cycle of beginning, ending, and transformation. Together, they tell a story of resilience, survival, and the relentless pursuit of being unforgettable.

In every life, I'll share the lessons, the moments that shaped me, and the people who showed me that even when life changes everything, you can still begin again.

A younger colleague, Catherine Bogdanski, once told me that leaders in the Independent Living Movement often repeat sayings and lessons I've shared over the years, what she affectionately calls "Theo-isms." At first, I laughed. But the more I thought about it, the more I realized she was right. Throughout my journey, I've carried not just stories, but truths I've wanted to pass on forged in struggle, humor, and hope.

So, Catherine, here's your credit: thank you for naming my Theo-isms. You'll find plenty of them in these pages.

This is not just the story of my life. It's a story about movement, community, and what it means to start over again and again.

Enjoy the journey.

Part I – My First Life: The Able-Bodied Experience

Chapter 1: Grandma's Cookies

I remember the day we moved in with Grandma. The Braddy family was always on the move, packing up from one place and starting again in another. We never owned the land we lived on. We were sharecroppers, working fields that belonged to white folks, always under their watch, always at their mercy.

I never fully knew Grandma's arrangement, but her house felt different. It felt safe. For the first time, it seemed like we had a home that was truly ours, even if it wasn't.

And then there were the cookies. Grandma had a way of turning the simplest things into gifts that stayed with you. Her cookies weren't just flour, sugar, and butter. Each one was a message: you matter, you are seen, you are unforgettable. Every time she placed one in my hand, it was like she was pulling me out of the shadows, reminding me that I counted.

I needed that. My older brother, born just before me, received all the attention. He was light-skinned, and in those days, that seemed to make him shine brighter in other people's eyes. I hated how he was favored, how the world seemed to treat him like he mattered more than me.

I'll never forget one night when we fled under the cover of darkness. I was probably 7 years old. My father had sharecropped for a corrupt sheriff who treated us like slaves, especially brutal to my dad. That night, we escaped, carrying nothing but desperation and hope. We walked for miles, leaving the county behind.

In the cover of darkness, my light-skinned brother was carried, held close, while I was made to walk. It was as if they forgot about me.

That moment burned into me. I was always the one left standing, waiting to be noticed.

It was then that something deep inside me formed: the need to be unforgettable. To stand out. To make sure the world couldn't pass me by.

And though that need would change over time, it never fully left me. It became part of who I am.

Chapter 2: Dad's Dimes

When my dad came home from work, his hands rough from the sawmill, he often reached into his pocket and pulled out a dime just for me. To most people, ten cents isn't much. But to a little boy longing to be seen, it was everything.

I would clutch that shiny coin like treasure and race off to buy a big bag of cookies, the kind that reminded me of Grandma's love. But the cookies weren't the real gift. The dime itself was.

Each time he placed it in my hand, I felt noticed. Important. Connected. In that small gesture, he was telling me I mattered.

That dime made me rich, not in money, but in love. Rich in the knowledge that, at least in my dad's eyes, I was unforgettable.

Chapter 3: A Night I'll Never Forget

I was only 8 years old when I learned my dad had died. The news came not in words I fully understood, but in the way the house shifted that night. Suddenly, everyone was moving, scrubbing, cleaning, preparing, as if tidying up could somehow hold back the storm that had already broken.

I didn't understand death, not really. But I understood enough to know that something permanent had happened, something that would change us forever. My dad, the man who handed me dimes with calloused hands, the man who made me feel rich with love, was gone.

They told us it was tuberculosis. Maybe it was. Or perhaps it was something else. In the 1960s, Black men in the South didn't get much investigation when they died. Causes of death were stamped onto certificates like afterthoughts. Questions went unanswered, and injustices were quietly buried alongside the bodies.

What I do know is this: that night stayed with me. The confusion. The heaviness in the air. The way the grown-ups carried both grief and silence left me with more questions than comfort.

Even now, all these years later, I can still feel the weight of that night pressing against me. It was my first real encounter with loss, and it marked me in ways I couldn't see then but understand now.

It was the night I realized how quickly love can vanish, and how deeply absence can shape a life.

Chapter 4: Brother Gone, Brother Returned

My brother Johnny was the wild one. Everyone knew it. Where I was cautious, he was bold. Where I tried to stay in line, he tested every boundary he could find. He had a fire in him that both scared and fascinated me.

One day, he pushed too far. Trouble found him, or maybe he went looking for it. Either way, Johnny was gone. Sent away to detention, locked up for choices that seemed bigger than either of us could understand at the time. I never understood the unfairness. He was sent away because a white man said he stole a few coins.

The house felt empty without him. Even though he often stole the spotlight, his presence filled a room. When he left, it was as if a hole had opened in our family. I missed him, but I also carried a mix of emotions I couldn't name back then. I was angry at him for leaving, confused about why life kept taking people away from me, and afraid about what might happen next.

And then, just as suddenly as he was gone, Johnny came back. Older, harder, and different. There was a distance in his eyes, a kind of knowing that comes only from living through things you can't explain to others.

We were brothers, but something had shifted. His time away carved a space between us that never fully closed. I still loved him, still looked up to him in my own way, but I also sensed that life had already placed us on two very different paths.

That was the first time I realized how quickly the people you count on can disappear and how, when they return, they are never quite the same.

Chapter 5: Losing My Brother

It is always too hot in the summer, living in Wadley, Georgia. One of my favorite things to do was swimming. I was good at it.

In Wadley, we didn't have a community pool. We swam in lakes, different ones throughout the city. Often, we snuck into private lakes. It was fun being chased out of these lakes; usually, the owners didn't mind, but they ran us off when it became bothersome. They knew it was too hot.

One of my biggest regrets was asking my older brother, Johnny, to come swimming with us on a particular day. I begged him. I wanted to reconnect with him, and this was my chance. He drowned that day.

I watched as he went under, waiting for him to return to the surface. He never did. His was the first dead body I saw as rescue divers pulled him out of the lake, and he lay there lifeless.

For years, I carried the weight of his death, thinking it was my fault. Maybe if I hadn't asked, he would still be alive. The guilt stayed with me for a long time. I lost my brother again, but this time it was forever.

Chapter 6: The Knife Fight

My mom and stepdad fought a lot, especially when they had been drinking. I hated it. One night, it got really bad; he hit her hard, and she pulled a knife on him. He grabbed it from her, and in that moment, I did something I will never forget.

I got in between them and grabbed his hand, trying to stop him. But as they struggled, the knife slipped, cutting into my hand deeply.

My mom then said something that has stayed with me to this day, "Never interfere in grown folks' business." After that, I stayed out of it. I never tried to protect her again.

This left me feeling a sense of betrayal. How could she not see I was left with no other choice but to step in? She was my mom!

Chapter 7: The Tire Jack Incident

One afternoon, I was helping my stepdad change a tire. To me, it wasn't just about the tire; it was about proving myself. I wanted him to see me, to know that I could be useful and handle responsibility. I watched every move he made, eager to be part of it.

In the middle of our work, I heard my mother's voice calling from inside the house. She needed me for something. But I didn't answer. I didn't move. I pretended not to hear her. I was afraid that if I left, I would miss out on my chance to learn, to prove that I belonged at my stepdad's side.

Then it happened. The tire jack slipped. In an instant, the rim came crashing down, smashing my finger beneath its weight.

The pain was sharp, searing, but the lesson was sharper.

That moment taught me something I have carried ever since: sometimes, in our eagerness to push forward, we ignore the voices of wisdom calling us back. And when we do, life has a way of teaching us the hard way.

Chapter 8: The Candy Caper

I loved my job at the neighborhood store. It gave me a little money, a little purpose, and a sense of pride. But one day, I made a mistake that nearly cost me more than I bargained for.

I told my friends that the store owner always left a window open. It was meant as casual talk, but words have a way of becoming actions. Before long, we had a plan in place. We slipped in at night and stole some candy.

Everything went smoothly at first. We were quiet, quick, and feeling bold. But then headlights cut through the dark, a cop car rolling down the street. Our hearts jumped into our throats. We bolted, running as fast as our legs could carry us, and somehow made it home in one piece.

Or so we thought.

Later that night, the sheriff himself showed up at our house. I froze in my bed, pretending to be asleep, but I saw the glimpse of his gun as he walked past me. He questioned my stepdad, asking where I had been. Without hesitation, my stepdad gave me an alibi. "He's been home all night," he said.

The sheriff left, and the house went quiet again. When I finally confessed to my stepdad what we had done, he just shook his head and let out a laugh. "You all were foolish," he said. "If you're going to steal something, at least steal food."

That night, I learned my lesson. I never stole again.

Chapter 9: The Mud Hole

People in our neighborhood called our little group of friends a "gang." We weren't a gang, not really. We were five kids who grew up together, who played from sunrise to sundown. We knew every shortcut, every empty lot, every place a game of basketball, football, or baseball could be played. Those were the best days: walking home after a game, laughing, dribbling, arguing about who hit the buzzer-beater or hit the ball hardest.

One afternoon, we had played a pickup game a good distance from home. It took us about an hour to walk back, cutting through parts of town that weren't ours. Wadley, in those days, was the segregated deep South, a place where lines were drawn and you learned fast which side you were supposed to be on.

On the way home, a yard sign stopped us dead: FREE PUPPIES. Who wouldn't look? We huddled up like conspirators and decided one of us would knock and ask. Kids being kids, curiosity was stronger than caution.

Before we reached the porch, a giant white man threw open his screen door and screamed at us, "What you little niggers doing in my yard?" His voice was loud and angry. We answered back, stupid and brave, "We want to see the free puppies." Then he spat words I still hear: "Ain't no free puppies for you niggers."

Someone tried to save face and shouted, "We don't want any anyway!" That only made him angrier. He said, "Wait, I'm gonna get my shotgun." Nobody gonna wait for somebody to get a shotgun. We bolted.

We ran like our lives depended on it. When we looked back, he was in his truck, chasing us. His tires spun and threw up dust. My friends ran into the sawmill, a maze of stacked lumber and shadowed walkways, and disappeared like a trick. I was the youngest and, for once, my small legs kept pace. But in the scramble, I lost sight of them. I was alone.

I ran until my lungs burned, and then I saw it: a wooden conveyor, raised high with a little dugout beneath it. It looked like the perfect hiding spot. I dove headfirst into the hole, wedging myself in, convinced I was invisible. Of course, I wasn't. My butt stuck out like a beacon.

The man found me. He stood over that hole, shotgun in hand, and bellowed, "Come out of there, nigger!" I crawled out, crying. He pointed the gun at my face and said, "If you niggers ever come up in my yard again, I'll stomp a mud hole up your asses."

I said, "Yes, sir," and ran.

Later, when we all met up and laughed nervously about it. I had never heard that phrase. It was the first time: stomp a mud hole in your ass, and I never forgot it.

The memory stayed with me not because of the words themselves but because of what they meant: the ordinary, everyday danger of being Black in the deep south.

Theo-ism: *If you're going to hide in a hole, make sure your butt is covered.*

Chapter 10: First Heartbreak

Marilyn was my first real girlfriend, and she was a few years older than I was. I was head over heels, as they say. But one day, she broke up with me, and my whole world shattered.

It was just puppy love, but the pain felt real. I guess I was equating it to other losses. I had lost my brother and my father, too.

I cried a lot. The pain was real to me, and it felt like it would never end. It wasn't until my best friend talked me through it that I started to feel better.

It was my first real taste of the heartache of love. As I reflect now, I believe it is important for us as adults to recognize pain is real for young teenagers.

Chapter 11: The Internship – My first glimpse of disability

In tenth grade, I signed up for a business class internship. Each student was assigned to a local business to get some real-world experience. While some classmates went to offices or stores, I was placed at a nursing home.

At first, I didn't think much of it. I figured it would be routine, walking the halls, helping where I could, maybe talking to a few residents.

One day, as part of my duties, I was asked to go room to room and spend time with the residents. I walked in and out of several rooms without much thought until I stepped into one that stopped me cold.

There, lying in the bed, was a young girl. She couldn't have been no more than eighteen. She was beautiful, unmistakably so. Her presence was startling in a place where I expected only the elderly and frail.

Curiosity got the best of me, so I struck up a conversation. Her warm smile made me

feel comfortable, and I quickly discovered that she was a quadriplegic. At the time, I didn't fully understand what that meant. All I knew was that she couldn't move her arms or legs. She told me she was paralyzed. Even then, the word felt heavy, though I couldn't grasp the full weight of it.

She was kind, easy to talk to, and before long, I found myself feeling both drawn to her and pitying her at the same time. She was beautiful, and yet I could only see what she had lost. Still, in those moments, we became friends.

At the end of my internship, I promised her I would come back to visit. I never did. Life moved on, and I let that promise fade.

I have never forgotten her, though. Not her face, not her smile, not the way she made me think differently about people living with paralysis, long before I would face it myself. Looking back, I wonder what that friendship could have taught me if I had kept my word.

Chapter 12: The Coach's Favorite

By the time I reached 10th grade, things were looking up. The football coach took a liking to me and made me his assistant.

Anytime he needed something, I got to skip class and help him out. This made me feel important, as if I were somebody.

I recall that feeling even now, being singled out by him. The coach said I played with a lot of heart and toughness. It was like something you see in these sports movies today, but it was real life to me in 1975.

Chapter 13: Game Night Glory

One night, I played one of my best games with the junior varsity basketball team. I left the gym tired but proud, and I didn't think much more about it. I figured it was just another game, one that would fade away like all the rest.

The next morning, I climbed onto the school bus, still half-asleep and carrying my books. As I walked past, the bus driver stopped me. She smiled and said, "Great game last night. I didn't know you could play like that."

I froze. For a second, I didn't know what to say. I hadn't expected anyone outside my teammates to notice. But in that small moment, I felt like a star, like someone had finally seen what I had to give.

It's amazing how just a few words can lift you higher than any trophy.

Chapter 14: She Picked Me

There was this girl in school, a popular 11th grader who all the older boys wanted to date. Her name was Shirley. She was popular, cute, and intelligent.

I don't know why, even to this day, but she picked me, a 10th grader, to be her boyfriend.

It was one of the best feelings I've ever had, walking around school knowing that someone like her chose me. It made me feel great, like I mattered in a big way.

It was one part of my life that felt like everything was coming together perfectly. I was becoming a jock and had a popular upper-class girlfriend. It couldn't get any better.

It never did.

Part II – My Second Life: The Disabled Experience

Chapter 1: The Day It Happened

April Fools' Day, 1975.

The irony of that date has never left me. A day known for pranks, laughter, and harmless tricks was the day my world broke open.

It was around three o'clock in the afternoon, the first day of football practice. I had been waiting for this moment all year. Sports were my heartbeat, basketball first, football a close second. Baseball had its place too, but nothing stirred me quite like the roar of the game, the rhythm of the plays, and yes, the eyes of the cheerleaders who cheered us on.

For a fifteen-year-old Black boy in Georgia, football meant more than competition; it meant belonging, pride, and the promise of being unforgettable.

I sprinted to practice that day, my chest filled with excitement. My coach often called me fearless, and I believed him. It wasn't just praise, it was proof that I was seen.

I suited up in oversized, hand-me-down pads and scuffed equipment. Nothing was new, but it didn't matter. It was mine, and I wore it like armor.

That afternoon, I lined up at left linebacker. Beside me was my childhood friend, Danny, a white boy I had grown up with, playing in the dirt lots and makeshift fields of Wadley.

Together, we were a wall. Our relationship was like a scene from the movie, The Titans, where Denzel Washington plays Coach Boone, where the iconic line of a back-and-forth between the characters of Bertier and Big Ju: Bertier says, "Left side!" and Big Ju responds, "Strong side!", we both were linebackers. We lived for the sound of a good hit, that sharp, satisfying crack when shoulder met shoulder, a kind of music only athletes understand.

The scrimmage was intense and then came the play I'll never forget: a quarterback sneak. I saw it forming, like slow motion. This was my moment. I lowered myself, ready to strike, ready to stop him before he crossed the line. In my mind, I could already hear the coach's praise, see the pride on his face.

I lunged.

But my foot slipped. My body pitched forward, off-balance but determined. I wasn't going to miss. I hit the quarterback head-on.

At first, there was no pain. Instead, there was a strange floating sensation, as though I were suspended in the air, balanced on the face guard of my helmet. I tried to move, but nothing.

My body didn't respond. I could hear voices, teammates gathering around me, their words sharp with fear.

"Coach! Coach!" someone yelled.

Coach ran over, breathless. He knelt beside me, his voice steady but urgent.

"You okay, son?"

"I can't move, Coach. What happened?" My voice cracked with confusion but not fear, not yet.

"Be still," he said firmly.

No problem. I couldn't move anyway.

Lying there on the field, I felt the world shift. At first, I thought it was temporary. Maybe I had the wind knocked out of me. I had been through that before. But as the minutes passed, something inside told me this was different.

The coach and a few teammates carefully turned me onto my back. Wrong move.

The second my body shifted, pain exploded, screaming pain that tore through me with a force I had never felt before. I cried out, the sound filling the field.

That was the moment. The moment my second life began.

Chapter 2: The Ambulance Rides

The Wadley Wildcats. That was our high school football team, and before I ever put on the uniform, I knew what it felt like to be swept up in the excitement.

At rallies, the band would play, the crowd would roar, and when one upperclassman hit that trumpet solo on "It's Just My Imagination" as the players charged onto the field, the whole school went wild.

I wanted to be one of those players, the ones everyone was cheering for running on the field. And finally, I was.

But I never made it to a rally. I never ran onto the field to the sound of that trumpet.

Instead, I had my first ride in an ambulance.

At first, I thought it was no big deal. My injury hurt, but I figured it would make for a funny story to tell my teammates later. I even thought of it as an adventure, something to laugh about once I was back on the field.

But there was no laughing, no joking, and no going back to that field. That ride marked the end of football for me.

Not long after, I found myself in another ambulance. This time, it was different. The doctor told my mom the hospital in Louisville wasn't equipped to handle my injury. I had to be rushed one hour away to Doctor's Hospital.

I could feel the seriousness in the air. Everyone around me was moving quickly, and machines were connected to me. Two attendants stayed by my side, asking me questions and keeping me talking. I talked nonstop, partly to stay calm, partly because I was terrified of the silence.

The ride only took an hour, but for a 15-year-old kid lying on that stretcher, it felt like forever.

My first ambulance ride ended one dream. My second ambulance ride marked the beginning of a whole new life.

Chapter 3: The Screws That Caused Pain, Relieved Pain

I remember being rushed through the emergency room. I had never felt anything like that before. The pain was so sharp that I had never experienced anything like it, and it felt unbearable. Worse than what I felt when my teammates turned me over on the football field.

I knew it was serious. Everyone around me was moving fast, talking over me, never to me. They just did things.

I kept hearing the words "Stryker frame," but I didn't know what they meant. I would soon find out.

They carefully transferred me onto what I thought was a narrow examination table. Later, I learned it was a Stryker frame. Again, no one explained a thing. They just moved me like a piece of equipment.

Then a lady quickly shaved both sides of my head. Panic shot through me. I was still trying to understand what was happening when I heard the whirring of a drill.

My whole body went alert, and panic overwhelmed me. I felt something cold being rubbed onto my temples, but I didn't know it was iodine then.

And then it happened. Without warning, a hole was drilled into the side of my head. Before I could process the first, the second came. Next came the screws, bolts twisted straight into my skull. The pain was indescribable. I screamed out loud. It was pain stacked on pain.

Then I heard the words: "Connect the weights." I swear, it was like night and day. The moment the weights were attached to the bolts in my head, my broken neck pulled back into alignment. The pain vanished, at least the neck pain did. I was okay with that for sure.

Later, I learned that the bolts were part of a pulley system designed to hold my neck in place while it healed. In that moment, I only knew relief. God was merciful, and eventually I passed out.

When I woke up, the lights above me were blinding. Nurses were still working. No one explained.

Someone said, "We need to turn him." They fitted the top half of the frame over me and tightened it down until I could only see through a small cutout for my eyes. Two women took positions, one at the top, one at the bottom, and in unison they counted, "One, two, three," and flipped me over.

Suddenly, I was staring at the floor. Blood, my blood, covered it. "Is that my blood?" I screamed, panicking like the 15-year-old kid I was. No one answered.

I stayed on that Stryker frame for months. It could flip me from back to front to prevent pressure sores, but all I saw day after day was the ceiling, then the floor. Ceiling. Floor. Ceiling. Floor. Those images are burned into me as much as the screws themselves.

Theo-ism: *Sometimes the very thing that hurts the most is what you need!*

Chapter 4: A Visit from Coach

This chapter is short because the visit itself was short, but its impact has lasted a lifetime.

That year, my coach and I had built a strong bond, both on and off the football field. I wasn't just another player to him. I became his assistant, the one he called on during the school day when he needed something. Sometimes I would tell my teachers, "Coach needs me," and they would let me go without question. It felt good to be trusted and needed.

So, when I was lying in the Stryker frame, it was him I wanted to see. And eventually, he walked in. He carried the same strong, steady look I had always known him for, but that day, it felt different. His face seemed heavier, like the strength he wore so naturally was straining under the weight of what he had to tell me.

He looked at me and said, "Son, this is serious." Somehow, he already knew what was racing through my mind. Then he said the words that cut through everything: "You won't be able to play football again. You broke your neck. You're paralyzed."

That was the last time I ever saw my coach.

Later in life, I learned he had been asked to break the news to me. But in that moment, it didn't matter who sent him. What mattered was that the man I trusted, the man who had believed in me, was the one to tell me the truth that would change everything.

Theo-ism: *The hardest truths hurt less when they come from someone who believes in you.*

Chapter 5: My New Home: Doctor's Hospital

At Doctor's Hospital, the doctors didn't offer much hope. They told me straight: my life expectancy wouldn't stretch beyond my twenties. I carried that weight quietly, tucked in the back of my mind. I never shared it, but it never left me. No one ever knew I kept track of the years I lived, waiting for my pending death. I believed the doctors.

In the early months at Doctor's Hospital, a neighborhood friend named Rick brought me a radio. He probably thought it was just a small gesture, but it became my lifeline.

The songs of the seventies filled the lonely days and long nights when I lay paralyzed, unable to move. Some songs made me cry. Others made me smile. In those quiet, still hours, especially late at night, the music gave me a place to go when my body couldn't. Even now, when I hear a seventies song, I drift back to those hospital nights in 1975.

Rick never knew what that radio meant to me. I hope one day I get the chance to tell him. **Thank you, Rick!**

My family visited when they could. My brother, just a few years older than me, even took time away from school to be with me. But more often than not, the hospital staff became my family.

One nurse in particular stood out. Funny enough, I later learned she was related to the girl who broke my heart in my first life.

Her name was Connie, and she showed me kindness in a way I've never forgotten. She brought me candy, not just once, but often, and taped the bars all around the walls of my room so I could see them. Whenever I wanted one, she would point, I would say yes, and she would then bring it to me.

It may have seemed like a small thing, but when you're fifteen and paralyzed, that kind of kindness is everything.

Years later, during my third life, I went back home and searched for Connie. I found her. And I finally got to say the words I had carried with me all those years: **thank you, Connie!**

Theo-ism: *Sometimes the smallest kindness becomes the greatest medicine.*

Chapter 6: Warm Springs

After my time at Doctor's Hospital, I thought I would finally go home. But instead, I was told I would be transported to Warm Springs Rehabilitation in Warm Springs, Georgia.

My family couldn't travel with me; we were dirt poor. In fact, back home, you could literally see the ground through gaps in the floor of our little shack. No one could afford the trip.

When I arrived, I was surprised to find that Warm Springs was filled with people of all ages and all kinds of disabilities.

At just fifteen, I had never seen anything like it. I was sitting in a manual wheelchair for the first time, fitted with what they called "quad wheels", small knobs on the rims that allowed me to push myself short distances. It was slow and awkward, but as the doctors explained, it would help me regain my strength.

I wasn't alone, but lonely. I was surrounded by people, but I felt lonely. Still, seeing others with severe disabilities gave me an odd perspective. As strange as it sounds, I felt lucky, lucky even with my diagnosis: a C4–C5 quadriplegic.

I now understood what that meant. My neck had been broken, my spinal cord was injured at that level, leaving me paralyzed below that injury level. Surgeons had taken a piece of bone from my hip and put it into my neck with a wire to stabilize it. That is where all the blood came from when I freaked out on the Stryker Frame.

My time at Doctor's Hospital gave my body the chance to heal, but Warm Springs gave me something else: the knowledge that there were others like me and even worse than me.

Within weeks, I met someone who would change my life, a young Black woman named Kate Gainer. It was lust at first sight. She was older, confident, and years later, she told me she thought of me as her "handsome young boy." For me, it was more than attraction; it was validation. She could have chosen anyone, but she chose me. I felt again unforgettable.

Everyone at Warm Springs noticed. Even the orderlies who worked with the residents seemed jealous. Rumors spread, but Kate and I didn't care. We were the "it couple" of Warm Springs.

Kate was already an advocate, and she encouraged me to be bold, to have courage, to speak up. She helped plant the seeds of the advocate and national leader I would later become.

When my rehab came to an end, the pull toward home was stronger than the pull to stay. I went back to my shack, and I only saw Kate once more in my third life. By then, she was married and had a son.

For those who may not recognize the name, yes, that's Kate Gainer. She became a nationally known disability rights advocate, making major changes in Georgia and on a national level. She was instrumental in the early days of the Independent Living Movement, though, like many Black advocates and advocates of color, her contributions were often overlooked.

Do yourself a favor: look her up. Here's one of my favorite speeches of hers: (https://www.youtube.com/watch?v=pUrs5Ar-PkY). Every time I hear it, I tear up with memories.

In 2024, at the National Council on Independent Living (NCIL) Conference, Kate was honored with the President's Award for her outstanding contributions to Independent Living and disability advocacy. Seeing her recognized was one of my proudest moments.

A full circle has happened a few times in my life. Warm Springs represented one of those full circles for me.

Franklin D. Roosevelt, the 32nd President diagnosed with polio in 1921, had come to Warm Springs seeking healing in its mineral waters. In 1927, he purchased the resort and turned it into the Warm Springs Foundation, one of the first rehabilitation centers in the U.S.

It became a place not only for physical recovery, but also for community and solidarity among people with disabilities. Roosevelt's experience there shaped his empathy and policies toward people with disabilities for the rest of his life.

I know that I am jumping ahead of the storyline, a little here, but this connection is significant.

Decades later, after I became Executive Director of NCIL, I received an email from Mary E. Dolan, Co-Founder and Executive Director of the FDR Memorial Legacy Committee. The FDR Memorial Legacy Committee was created to make sure FDR's story, especially his life as a disabled leader is told.

She reminded me that when the committee first formed, it operated under NCIL's 501(c)(3) for two years.

Mary invited me to speak at the 26th anniversary of the FDR wheelchair statue being added to the memorial, the result of decades of advocacy by the disability community.

When I told Mary that I had once been a rehab patient at Warm Springs, the very facility FDR created she was amazed. For me, it was a full 360 moment. Warm Springs gave me not only rehabilitation, but also a sense of identity, belonging, and purpose. Without that experience, I would not be the man I am today.

Chapter 7: Going Home: Shack, Faith and Healing

It was finally time. After so long in hospitals and rehab, I was told I could go home.

When I broke my neck on the football field, I was rushed away in an ambulance, away from my teammates, my high school friends, my teachers, and my community. I never saw many of them again.

As I sit here writing this, it hits me: I don't even remember how I got back home. You would think that moment would be burned into me, but it's gone.

I do remember being carried into my little shack and placed in the room I shared with my older brother, and yes, the light-skinned one. They set me down in a hospital bed, donated by someone kind enough to give it to me. I was grateful. I needed it. By then, I had grown used to hospital beds.

The shack was still home. I was glad to see it, but fear quickly settled in. I no longer had nurses or orderlies trained to care for me. Now it was my family, my mother and brother, who had to figure out how to meet all my needs. I had to teach them everything, step by step. I couldn't see how it would work. Soon, I was proven right.

At first, the town buzzed with talk. Wadley was small, maybe 2,200 people, and word spread quickly.

I became "the boy who broke his neck." Before long, a group of elders from the local church came to my bedside. They said I needed prayer. They laid their hands on me and shouted prayers of healing, telling me that if I had enough faith, I would get up and walk again.

I wanted to believe them. When they left, I laid there, staring at my body, trying to will even a single toe to move. Day after day, night after night, I prayed and believed. And when nothing happened, I blamed myself. My faith must not have been strong enough.

That wound of believing God had denied me because of my lack of faith, stayed with me for years. For much of my second life, I turned away from the church because of the harm those Elders had done.

Meanwhile, life at home grew harder. My mom and brother did all they could, but the shack had no indoor plumbing, no ramps, barely any space. I stayed in bed most of the time, far too long.

Eventually, a visiting social worker convinced my mother I needed to be placed in a nursing home. By that time, even I agreed.

And then life came full circle. Remember the beautiful eighteen-year-old quadriplegic girl I met during my first life, the one I promised to visit but never did? I ended up in the very same nursing home, in the very same room.

Another full circle of life. Isn't life funny?

Theo-ism: *Sometimes home can never be home again.*

Chapter 8: Back to School

I almost left this part out. I don't like thinking about it. But if I'm telling the truth about my journey, I need to share it.

After my accident, after coming home, I tried to go back to school. I still remember that first day.

The regular school bus pulled up to my stop, just like it always had. But this time it was different. I was in a manual wheelchair, and for the first time in history, at least in my little corner of Georgia. They had to figure out how to get a wheelchair and me onto that old, inaccessible bus.

They brainstormed, fumbled, and finally decided someone would carry me on while my classmates sat on the bus staring, impatient and curious. I can still feel their eyes on me. By the time I finally got inside, humiliation had already set in.

And the day didn't get better. I sat in class, silent. No one spoke to me. Not one friend. The teacher tried to be kind, but kindness can only go so far when the rest of the room pretends you don't exist.

When I got home that afternoon, I begged my mom not to make me go back. To my surprise, she didn't. That day became my last day of school. I never saw my classmates again, well except one: Albert.

There was one exception. Only one friend came to see me after I got home.

Just one. And I had been a pretty popular kid before my accident.

His name was Albert Young. We had grown up together since kindergarten.

To this day, I can call Albert up, and it's like we never missed a beat. We would pick up right where we left off.

I guess we all have that one or two friends who stay the course, no matter what changes.

Albert was different. My disability didn't change how he saw me.

He figured out quickly what others couldn't, that I was still the same Theo.

Years later, after I had moved to Pennsylvania, it had been nearly twenty years since I had heard from him.

Then one day, out of nowhere, he found me.

He called and said, "I'm coming up to see you."

And that's exactly what he did.

He jumped in his car in Wadley, Georgia, and drove twelve hours straight to Harrisburg, Pennsylvania.

When we saw each other, it was like time hadn't passed at all. We reconnected instantly.

Since then, Albert has never stopped visiting, and we've never stopped talking.

Just a few months ago, he came to see me again. This time with his three kids, Ethan, Edwin and Carleigh. They call me Uncle Theo.

They laughed as I told them stories about their dad and me, mostly about how foolish we were back in the day. They loved it.

Thank you, Albert, for seeing Theo, not "disabled Theo."

Chapter 9: The Nursing Home Experience

In the deep South, when a professional white person told you something, you listened. It was an unwritten law. From an early age, this was drilled into me. I saw the white sheriff talk to my grown father like a child, and my father did what the "high sheriff" told him to do.

So, when the white social worker told my mom I needed to be placed in a nursing home, she obeyed. I wasn't asked, but strangely enough, I would have said yes. I had gotten used to nurses and orderlies, to being in an institutional setting after months in the hospital and rehab.

Let me say this now: a nursing home is no place for a fifteen-year-old teenager. Some things should never be experienced.

I was quickly moved in and immediately met with rules and requirements. The first thing drilled into you as a resident were the things you could not do.

There were visiting hours for friends and family. But I didn't have any friends come. Truthfully, I didn't want them to. Not after the silence I faced when I tried to go back to school. My family didn't visit that often either. I was mostly on my own, surrounded by extremely old and sickly residents.

I'll end this chapter quickly because I don't like recalling these memories. But one memory is seared into me forever.

It was the nights that were the worst. I usually had a room by myself, and during this time, I was alone.

Directly across the hall from me was an older male resident, very sickly. For some reason, only at night, he would yell out in pain. The screams were long, eerie, and relentless. At first, they frightened me. And when I say every night, I mean every single night!

"Help me, someone, please help me!" he cried, over and over, into the dark.

It got so bad that sometimes I would start yelling too, begging the staff to help him. The kind staff, the ones who liked me, would sometimes respond and attend to him. That gave me a little peace until I drifted off, only to be startled awake again by his screams.

This was my routine, night after night, until the man died.

And when he did... was it wrong for me to feel a sense of relief?

Chapter 10: My Family Saved Me

When I say my family saved my life, I mean it. They truly saved me.

I had been in a nursing home for about a year. You already know one of the stories that still haunts me, the man across the hall whose screams at night penetrated my spirit. That was just one memory among many. And I'll repeat it: a nursing home is no place for a fifteen-year-old!

We didn't have money. I've already said it; we were dirt poor. But my family saw what that place was doing to me. They saw my dilemma, and they refused to leave me there.

Led by my sisters, Annie Phillips and Gladys Braddy, they pulled their money together and planned my escape. Somehow, they managed to get me a plane ticket at a time when it wasn't easy to figure out such things and flew me to Harrisburg, Pennsylvania.

But there was another problem waiting. I would be living with Annie, and she lived in a three-story apartment.

I made the trip without incident, and upon arrival in Harrisburg, I was driven to my new home in Hall Manor. Anyone who knows Harrisburg is familiar with Hall Manor, a subsidized housing complex for low-income families.

Remember the movie, *The Man in the Window*? The apartment became my home. But the place I lived most of the time was a little room on the third floor, with a single window. For months, I was "the man in the window." I experienced life from behind the glass, watching the world move on without me.

The only times I left that room were when my two brothers came over to carry me down, like a baby, down three flights of stairs, so I could sit outside. Sometimes in the backyard. Sometimes in the front. Always looking for the sun. If you've read any of my social media reflections, you know I am a sun-gazer, even back then.

So much of my time with Annie was spent either at that third-floor window or outside in the sunlight. Those were my options, unless I had a doctor's appointment.

Even now, writing this brings back memories and emotions I've tucked away. Sometimes, it still makes me sad.

But here's what matters most: my family saved me. I don't know if they ever fully understood what they did for me, or how much it meant. But moving to Harrisburg and leaving that nursing home behind changed the course of my life. It set me on a new path. **Thanks, Fam!**

Chapter 11: Elizabethtown Hospital for Crippled Children

While living with my sister in Hall Manor, I was admitted to the Elizabethtown Hospital for Crippled Children, which is now known as Elizabethtown College. I remember calling it E-Town.

I honestly don't remember how I ended up there or ever agreeing to go. By then, I was seventeen, still young, and this was the start of something that would follow me for years: being the first black person or black disabled person in a lot of places.

That experience always came with a feeling I could never quite shake, the stares, the whispers that weren't really whispers, the quiet reminder that I didn't belong. It was different. It was uncomfortable. But it was also shaping me in ways I didn't yet understand.

Once again, I was left there on my own, away from my family. By this point, though, I had gotten used to it. I never blamed them. I knew they did what they could. Being on my own made me pay attention to people, to systems, to every small detail. I became a sponge, soaking up every experience. And at E-Town, there were plenty.

One of the first people I met there was the hairstylist. She was a kind, older white lady who looked genuinely nervous when they rolled me in for my first grooming appointment. She stared for a moment and then admitted, "I've never worked on a Black person's hair before."

I didn't mention that I had a huge afro. It was 1977, and for Black folks, the bigger the better. She looked at me, curious, almost fascinated, as she ran her fingers through my hair, laughing softly as if trying to figure it out.

Over time, we became friends. This was becoming a pattern in my life. People always seemed to like me once they got to know me. Eventually, I decided to relax my hair, which we called a "perm" back then. It turned out great. I called it my Elvis period.

However, my most meaningful experience at E-town came from an unexpected source, a staff member whose name I can no longer recall. He found out I had never graduated from high school.

Remember, I had begged my mother not to make me go back after my accident, and she hadn't. So, there I was, seventeen years old, with no diploma.

This man took an interest in me. He would stop by and challenge me, talk to me about my future. One day, he said, "Theo, you should get your GED. I will help you."

I laughed it off. "No way," I told him. "I can't do algebra. I will never pass."

He didn't let it go. He said, "You can. I will teach you." And he did. We worked hard, put in long hours, and faced lots of frustration, but I took that test and passed on the first try.

From that experience, I learned something that would stay with me forever: you can learn anything if you have the right teacher and the will to work hard.

Not all of my experiences there were good, though. E-town was also where I learned my first real lesson about power and helplessness, a lesson that planted the seed for my lifelong advocacy.

People often forget that young people with disabilities are still just that, young people. We want to stay up late, listen to music, talk, and laugh. We want freedom.

One evening, I wanted to stay up and listen to music. However, there was a head nurse at E-Town who stood out from the rest. Hard. Strict. All rules, no heart.

She came into my room around 7:00 p.m. and said, "Lights out. Bedtime."

I told her I wasn't ready, in the way only a teenager can say it. She turned around quietly and walked out. I thought I had won. I thought, cool, I get to stay up.

A few moments later, she returned with two large orderlies (male aides). Without a word, they grabbed my chair, rolled me roughly to the bed, lifted me, and threw me in. They threw the covers over and walked out. She stood there, silent, watching, making sure I understood.

That night, I got her message.

I wasn't in control. I didn't have any power.

That moment burned into me. It was the spark that lit my fire to fight for my rights and for the rights of every person who's ever been made to feel powerless.

Theo-ism: *If something affects you, it affects others like you, so fighting for yourself is fighting for others.*

Chapter 12: The Island of Misfits

One would think I would be finished with rehabilitation by now. But soon after leaving Elizabethtown Hospital for Crippled Children, I went on to another place called Johnstown Rehab.

I learned about it through the Office of Vocational Rehabilitation (OVR) (a state agency that helps people with disabilities prepare for, obtain, and maintain employment). At that time, I was just beginning to understand how the system worked, and with the help of others, I got connected to OVR.

I was around 18 or 19 years old, and this was where they sent people like me, young teenagers with disabilities who were ready for "training" to prepare for employment.

Johnstown, Pennsylvania, was historically known for its great flood. I remember thinking, 'Why in the world would they build a rehab center in a town famous for flooding?' To me, the place felt high up in the mountains, and I was already nervous about going.

However, when I arrived, I found it fascinating, a small town, quiet, surrounded by hills.

I was placed in the medical wing, the section for students whose disabilities were considered too severe to live independently. Those who could handle more of their daily care independently stayed in dorms.

I wanted so badly to be in those dorms to have a taste of freedom, not to have people watching over me 24/7. I didn't call it independent living back then, but that's exactly what I wanted.

Johnstown Rehab was different. There were people with every kind of disability you could imagine, physical, sensory, learning, cognitive, and from all across the country. We all fit in together.

If you remember the old Christmas movie Rudolph the Red-Nosed Reindeer, there was that "Island of Misfit Toys." That was Johnstown Rehab, the island of misfits.

All of us misfits were sent there to be "trained" for employment in the trades such as carpentry, electrical, etc. If you showed potential or anything close to "normal," you could also take classes in accounting, clerical work, or dental technology.

I started in clerical and accounting before settling on offset printing. Back then, that meant learning how to print business cards, letterhead, and stationery. I loved the darkroom, with its smell of ink, the quiet hum of the machines, and the sense of creation.

But deep down, my heart wanted more. I wanted to go to college.

When I told my OVR counselor that, he looked at me and said, "You're not college material."

I believed him. I never brought it up again.

I didn't realize it then, but I was being warehoused. The system didn't know what to do with people like me, so they gave us false hope, making us believe we were being prepared for "gainful employment," a phrase they often used at the time.

Although my time at Johnstown Rehab was full of adventure, I wouldn't feel right talking about all the things I took pleasure in back then, but I just want you to remember this: It is something decision makers often forget. Just because a young person has a disability or condition, or uses a wheelchair like me, we are still teenagers, and we do what typical teenagers do, regardless of the disability.

And it was being a typical teenager, which shortened my stay at Johnstown Rehab.

Remember, I lived in the medical wing, the place under constant watch. And if you remember my earlier experiences at E-Town, you know I had a history with nurses. Well, that history followed me here.

One night, I was coming back from the dorms after doing what teenagers do. A nurse came to help me transfer into bed. This time, I was actually ready for bed. I rolled my manual chair close, preparing for a quad transfer: that's when someone helps guide your body safely from your wheelchair into bed.

As I pulled off the armrest, I heard something drop to the floor. The sound hit me hard.

I knew exactly what it was. I had hidden a marijuana cigarette inside a mini cassette tape case. I prayed that the case wouldn't pop open. But of course, it did. The joint rolled out right in plain sight.

The nurse looked down. I looked down. Then we both looked up at each other.

She sighed. "You know I've got to report this, don't you?"

And I said, "You gotta do what you gotta do."

The next morning, right at 8:30 a.m., when the administrative offices opened, I heard my name over the intercom: "Will Theo Braddy please report to his counselor's office!"

It was the same counselor who had told me I wasn't college material.

Remember the movie, The Green Mile. Tom Hank played the prison guard when he always walked the mile with the prisoner right before their execution. So, like the Green Mile, I rolled down this very long hallway to his office (yes, I'm a movie nerd).

And just like that, I was kicked out of Johnstown Rehab.

Looking back, it's funny how one mistake can lead to the right kind of freedom.

By the way, Johnstown Rehab is now called the Hiram G. Andrews Center, and it operates as a community college.

Theo-ism: *This is not Theo-ism, but one of my favorite quotes by Louis L'Amour: "There will come a time when you believe everything is finished; that will be the beginning."*

The Game Changer

Let me take a commercial break to discuss the Office of Vocational Rehabilitation (OVR) a bit further.

I don't want anyone to be mistaken about how I feel regarding OVR.

OVR changed my life in extraordinary ways. They believed in and supported me when they saw I was determined.

They supported me through college at Edinboro University and later through graduate school at Temple University.

When I got my first professional job, OVR was still there. I needed a modified van to drive independently.

They didn't just help. They paid for the van modifications, not once, but multiple times over the years, until I was financially stable enough to no longer need their assistance.

That kind of commitment stays with you. It's probably why I've always been eager to give back and now serve on the PA State OVR Board. I know firsthand the power of what they do.

When I look back at my journey, I can honestly say that I have more than repaid their investment in me. They gave me the opportunity, and I have spent my life paying it forward.

The best thing about OVR's program is simple: they invest in people. That initial investment yields a greater return on investment, not just for me, but for the community.

Because of OVR, I became a tax-paying citizen in 1989, and I've been doing that ever since.

More importantly, I have been able to help others, open doors for people with disabilities, make systems more accessible, and ensure that others have the same opportunities I was given.

There's no greater dividend than that!

The Great Equalizer

Another life-changing support system that originated from OVR and Community Waiver is the Attendant Care Program, which I have utilized throughout my life and career.

I often call attendant care "The Great Equalizer." And that's precisely what it is.

Because of my paralysis and dependence on a complex motorized wheelchair, there are certain things I physically cannot do, such as getting in and out of bed, dressing, bathing, and managing daily routines.

My attendants help me with those tasks so I can focus on what I do best: leading, serving, and advocating.

Attendant care allows me to compete, contribute, and live with independence. It doesn't remove my disability, but it removes barriers that keep me from participating fully in life.

I honestly don't know where I would be without these services.

Over the years, I have had many attendants. Too many to name here, but they all hold a special place in my heart. So, to represent them all, I will mention two who are part of my life now:

Derrick "Peanut" Vines, whom I lovingly nicknamed Li Heifer Boy (his rapper's name I coined for him jokingly), and Chloe Harris, who came into my life like a burst of energy and light. She's exactly the kind of zeal I need at this stage in my life.

These two represent all attendants unnamed here. To all my attendants, past and present. **Thank you!**

You do not receive the credit, recognition, or pay you deserve. But know this: I see you! I appreciate you!

And I will always fight for you, because you are the reason people like me can live, work, and thrive in a world not built or designed for us.

Chapter 13: Early One Morning

I have often told young people that my favorite part of the day is the early morning.

Even in the Bible, great things happened early in the morning. It's a time of creation.

There's something about that time, the quiet, the stillness, the sense that the world is just waking up, that fills me with peace and creativity.

That morning was no different. I was sitting outside in my wheelchair, sun gazing. Let me explain the need to sun gazed, since it is so key to my peace of mind. Most quadriplegics will tell you we love the warmth of the sun on our faces. For many of us, it's one of the few parts of our bodies that still feel everything. It is not affected by the spinal cord injury.

Back to the story. My brother and I were living together at the time, in apartment 501 at McClay Street Apartments, on the first level.

From where I sat, I could look straight across the playground that stretched through the middle of the complex, about fifty yards across to where the other buildings stood.

A good friend of mine lived over there, almost directly across from me. We were close.

Both of us are from Wadley, Georgia, our hometown.

That morning, as I sat there, I saw her come out of her apartment. She moved fast, jumped into her car, and drove off in a hurry. I remember thinking something must be wrong.

I thought about it all day until I finally saw her again that afternoon.

When she pulled in, I called over to her and asked, "Hey, where were you going in such a hurry this morning?"

She smiled and said, "Oh, I was running late for my class."

"What class?" I asked, curious.

"I'm taking classes at HACC," she said.

"What's HACC?"

"Harrisburg Area Community College."

"You go to college?" I asked, surprised.

"Yes," she said. "I just started."

I told her that it was awesome. We chatted for a bit and then went on with our day. But I couldn't stop thinking about what she said.

She was my friend. We hung out together. We came from the same place. And now she was in college.

Now, I couldn't shake what that OVR counselor had told me years earlier: "You're not college material."

But here was my friend, someone I knew I was just as smart as, going to college. Why her and not me?

Could that counselor have been wrong? Was it because I was Black? Or because I was in a wheelchair? Those questions haunted me. They circled around in my mind over and over again.

Finally, I had enough. I asked my friend more about how she got started. She told me what she did, how she applied, and what it took to achieve it.

And right then, something clicked.

Maybe it wasn't about me at all. Perhaps it was about him, the counselor, and what he believed about me.

Then I remembered what I had learned when I got my GED: that anyone can do anything if they have the proper support and are willing to put in the hard work.

I had passed that GED on my first try because someone believed in me. Maybe that was the missing piece, the counselor just didn't believe in me, or worse yet, I didn't believe enough in myself.

So, I took a chance. I filled out an application to Harrisburg Area Community College.

And I got accepted.

That morning started like any other, quiet, peaceful, and full of sunlight, as I often do, sun gazed.

But by the end of it, it had changed the direction of my life.

Theo-ism: *Use the negative things people say or believe about you as your greatest motivation.*

Chapter 14: Edinboro University – What Was I Thinking?

I was really good at this college thing. I surprised myself.

At HACC, I discovered a world I had never even known existed. It wasn't an island of misfits anymore. It was real life, classes, debates, friendships, and independence.

In fact, I was the only wheelchair user at HACC.

That first academic year went by fast. I even dipped my toe into a little advocacy work. When I realized the Student Union didn't have an automatic door, I started asking questions. Eventually, the administration agreed to install one. It was a small win, but it opened something inside of me. I was finding my voice.

For the first time, I began to understand that society wasn't built to accommodate people like me and that the problem wasn't necessarily me. It wasn't always about being carried or asking for help. Some barriers could simply be removed.

Now, OVR was proud of me, a young, Black man with a disability, succeeding in college. They made sure I knew it, too. I saw firsthand how OVR supported success. When you did well, doors opened. That made me even more determined to do better.

Because deep down, I knew people were waiting for me to fail. And I couldn't give them that satisfaction.

By this point, I had a new OVR counselor, not the one who told me I wasn't "college material."

This counselor was different. Supportive. When I told him I wanted to go to a four-year university, he didn't laugh or talk me out of it. He said, "Let's look at some options."

My first choice was Howard University. I even got accepted. However, when I visited, accessibility was a significant issue, not just a minor one. I realized I would be fighting uphill battles every day just to get into buildings.

Around that time, my OVR counselor told me about Edinboro State University in northwestern Pennsylvania. OVR had actually helped create a model program there for students with disabilities. They had accessible vans to get students to class through the brutal winters, and personal care attendants on staff to help with daily needs. It was a state-of-the-art setup.

I couldn't visit. It was six hours away, but the more I heard, the more it sounded like an opportunity I couldn't pass up. So, I took the leap.

I will never forget that drive to Edinboro. It was winter. All I could see were giant hills of snow everywhere. Big snow piles surrounded me. The wind whipped across the highway like something out of a movie.

And I remember pondering, what was I thinking?

But it turned out to be one of the best decisions I ever made.

Edinboro was everything I needed. Of course, there were challenges. There always are.

I was, once again, the first Black student with a disability in the program. Apparently, that was a big deal. I later learned that the administrators were nervous about how it would go.

They assigned a white graduate student to "keep an eye on me." Her name was Ann and let me take a moment to thank Ann.

Ann helped me through some tough times during my first few semesters there. She was only supposed to work with me for one semester, but we became friends, and she stayed connected even after finishing her graduate work. She was older, wiser, and a proud member of MENSA. **Thank you, Ann.** I will never forget you.

At HACC, I initially studied early elementary education. I wanted to be a teacher. But after a semester at Edinboro, I switched my major to social work. The social work students just "got" me. They were open-minded, passionate about people, and ready to change the world.

And like every social work student, I wanted to change the world too.

But that passion also led me straight into my first big controversy.

Edinboro's campus was beautiful, especially in the spring and summer. But that first winter semester was miserable. The snow never stopped. The "lake effect" from Lake Erie is no joke. It buried the whole town for months.

When summer came around, I wanted to take classes in the sunshine for once. But OVR told me they wouldn't pay for summer semesters.

That made no sense to me. They would pay during the worst snowstorms, when everything was buried under ice and snow, but not when it was finally nice enough to get around campus easily.

I didn't buy it.

By this point, advocacy was becoming my superpower. So, I wrote a letter, not just any letter, but to the Executive Director of OVR, which oversaw the funding. I laid out my case: why summer classes made sense, the advantages, the impact on students like me.

To my surprise, he wrote back.

He even said he wanted to visit the campus to talk with me in person. Maybe it was political, maybe it was public relations, but I didn't care. It was a chance to make my case.

I just didn't expect the fallout.

The Executive Director of the Disabled Students Program wasn't happy. The university president wasn't either. They worried I would jeopardize funding or embarrass the university. But all I wanted was to take summer classes.

Ultimately, the head of OVR visited. We talked and I presented my case, we took pictures, and that was that.

A few weeks later, too my surprise, I received a letter from him. They had revised their policy. Students with disabilities could now attend summer semesters as long as they maintained their grade point average (GPA).

That letter changed more than just my schedule. It changed policy statewide.

No one probably knows that to this day.

Before I graduated, I was named Outstanding Social Work Student of the Year, an honor chosen by the entire social work faculty. I also earned Advanced Standing for graduate school, which allowed me to complete my master's degree one semester early.

I chose Temple University in North Philadelphia.

I was so excited about attending graduate school that I didn't participate in my own graduation ceremony at Edinboro with my fellow classmates. That's one of the few decisions I still regret.

Chapter 15: Temple University — My MSW

I didn't take a break.

After graduating from Edinboro University in 1986, I attended Temple University in North Philadelphia.

Around that time, I began reflecting deeply on my journey. On how far I had come. I thought about being that 15-year-old kid who broke his neck and somehow survived. I didn't even know it was possible to survive a broken neck.

I thought about being poor, about losing both my parents so young. My mother had passed away too, around my 19th birthday.

I thought about my family, who refused to give up on me. I reflected on everything I had endured and everything I still wanted to accomplish.

I wasn't done yet.

But Temple wasn't Edinboro. It was different, bigger, faster, louder. Temple was international. Students came from all over the world to study there. And here I was, a young, Black C4 quadriplegic in a manual wheelchair, alone again, this time in North Philadelphia.

I had heard the stories about North Philly. And as much as I would like to say I was fearless, that wouldn't be true.

A young man I mentored recently told me when I shared my story, "You must be fearless." I smiled when he said that, but the truth is I was scared to death during this period.

Still, fear has never stopped me. It only pushed me harder.

By now, I understood that society's expectations for people with disabilities are painfully low. But those low expectations became my fuel. I was determined not just to meet them but to exceed them, for myself and for everyone like me.

That's when I started to realize my purpose. I was meant to be a trailblazer.

Theo-ism: Never lower the bar of expectations, but challenge others and yourself to rise to meet the bar of expectations.

The Cold Night

My first significant barrier at Temple came early. It was winter. It was cold, sharp, and unforgiving.

I was living in the graduate dorms and pushing my way back from a late class through the icy wind. When I reached the building, I realized I couldn't open the door. My hands were cold and getting numb, and the door was too heavy and slippery. I didn't have that problem in the warm days.

There I was, stuck outside, in the freezing dark.

I don't remember how long I waited, but it felt like forever, the cold bit through my clothes. My hands got numb. My breath turned to frost. I just sat there, hoping someone, anyone, would come by.

Finally, a student appeared and opened the door for me. I was grateful but humiliated.

To fully appreciate this incident, you need to know that I was interning at Temple Law School at the time under the supervision of Mary Hanna, the head of legal counsel.

Mary Hanna was awesome. She taught me so much. I almost changed my career path to become a lawyer because of her influence on me. **Thank you, Mary!**

The next day, during my supervision meeting at Temple Law School, I told my field instructor, Mary Hanna, what had happened.

Mary was extraordinary, sharp, compassionate, and fearless. She challenged me constantly.

When I told her my story, she was furious. "You can't just accept that," she said. Write the President of the University. Tell him exactly what happened."

It didn't take much convincing. Edinboro had already taught me what one letter could do.

So, I wrote the letter.

And like so many others before him, the President wrote back: "We'll look into it."

Weeks passed. Nothing changed.

Mary kept asking for updates, but she didn't intervene. She was teaching me that advocacy isn't about waiting for someone else to fix it. It's about learning to fight for yourself.

Chapter 16: My Tribe

Around the same time, I was taking a course called "Social Policy & Problems." The professor announced a major class project: we were to identify a social problem and develop a change plan.

I didn't have to look far for mine.

I told the class about my situation. How I couldn't get into my own dorm, how I had written the President, and how nothing had changed.

Something incredible happened next.

The professor and every student in that classroom decided to join my fight.

We organized a sit-in. Word spread across the social work department. On the chosen day, every class came to a halt. Professors, students, and everyone joined together and marched to the President's office.

We filled the hallway, chanting, holding signs, and demanding change.

Even now, all these years later, when I tell this story, I tear up. Because in that moment, for the first time in my life, I felt what it truly meant to belong.

They weren't fighting for me. They were fighting with me.

I had found my tribe.

We protested on a Friday. By Monday, the university had installed an automatic door with a push button at my dorm entrance.

From that day forward, I never had to wait outside in the cold again.

That door wasn't just a door. It was proof that change could happen when people stand together.

That was a life-changing moment for me.

I graduated from Temple University in 1988. This time, I made sure to attend my graduation ceremony. I wasn't going to miss rolling across that stage with my classmates and professors looking on.

I wanted to celebrate not just my degree, but also the community that had supported me along the way.

I was thankful to do it with my tribe.

Chapter 17: "Mr. Braddy, You Just Won a Championship: What's Next?"

You have probably seen the commercial. A team wins the championship, the star player gets asked, "Now that you've won the championship, what's next?" And with a big smile, they shout: "I'm going to Disney World!"

I hadn't won a Super Bowl and wasn't going to Disney World, but I had crossed my own finish line. I had just graduated from Temple University with a Master's degree in Social Work. I had the diploma in my hand. The question was the same: What's next?

One thing I had learned during my undergraduate years at Edinboro University, and then sharpened at Temple, was the importance of connecting with people.

I understood the power of picking up the phone, calling someone in leadership, and simply asking for an informational interview. Not for a job, not for favors, just to learn about their work, their agency, and their journey.

One of the first people I reached out to was Thomas Neuville, then the Executive Director of the Commonwealth Institute. Later, he would become Dr. Thomas Neuville, a respected professor at Millersville University. Before that, he had spent years running a Center for Independent Living in Denver.

That first conversation lasted only thirty minutes. However, it sparked a friendship that has endured for more than three decades.

Thomas stood beside me when I brought Ed Roberts to keynote the first conference I ever organized: "Becoming Your Own Best Advocate." Together, the three of us co-facilitated sessions that planted seeds for a generation of advocates.

Years later, when Thomas was teaching at Millersville, he designed a course with me in mind: Discrimination and Oppression of Persons with Disabilities. He recruited me to teach it as an adjunct professor. The class became one of the most popular on campus, so popular that it was always over-enrolled.

I taught it for years, proud to shape young minds who would carry this work forward.

Now, as I write my memoir, I still cherish the friendship Thomas, and I share. We still meet, still talk about everything, and still exchange wisdom. His insight has been a gift.

And it all began with a thirty-minute interview.

Oh, and yes, at the end of that interview, I asked him if there were any job opportunities. He smiled and told me no, nothing was available.

At the time, I thought I was leaving empty-handed. Looking back, I see it differently. The truth is, he gave me something far more valuable than a job: he gave me friendship.

Theo-ism: *Until you land that perfect job, volunteer.*

Part III – My Third Life: The Leader Within: Family & Community Leadership

Chapter 1: A Few Thoughts on Family Leadership

After I sang my way back into Roe's life and we remarried, things were different. God was doing a new thing in me. I was becoming a family leader.

Most of us start marriage without a good road map. If you had parents whose marriage you could model, you at least had something, but even then, there are no guarantees.

I didn't have a road map. The closest thing to that was the bible, and I was still learning it.

Chapter 2: Iron Sharpens Iron

We now had a church family. We remarried at East Shore Community Church, surrounded by our loved ones and our unwavering support, Pastor Clifford Ashe.

At East Shore, we saw how it could be done. We watched Pastor and his wife, Audree, live it. Everybody wanted a marriage like that.

Pastor loved Audree, both in word and in deed, and he challenged us to do the same with our wives.

He made the expectations practical: open car doors for your wives; open doors for any woman, anywhere.

Leadership can be taught and caught. We were taught, and we caught it. We were becoming mighty men.

"Iron sharpens iron" (Proverbs 27:17). That was our way, men and women sharpening each other. Most days, it worked beautifully. One day, it didn't.

Chapter 3: You Can't Do That!

One of the tasks we were encouraged to do as men included gathering and engaging in activities outside of the church to develop a stronger bond.

So, I invited another fellow member out to a movie. He agreed to go together. We were both professionals. He was an accountant, and I ran my own agency as CEO.

It made sense that we would have a lot in common and would hopefully develop a friendship.

Pastor was big on having accountability partners. He knew we would be more accountable to each other and have a greater chance of not falling back into the things that had gotten us into trouble in the first place.

It made sense. I even recall the movie being an action-adventure at the Colonial Park Mall.

At the time, it was overcrowded. Everyone was out to see this summer blockbuster, a sea of people in the mall. One could easily get misplaced if not paying close attention.

We went into the mall together, chatting it up, and were having a good time.

He was a funny guy, so we were laughing and joking about everything, and even making fun of other members of the church in a lighthearted way. Nothing mean-spirited.

We entered the mall and immediately commented on all the people. It was very crowded.

We went in and purchased tickets. We were early, so we had some time to kill, so I suggested we browse around the mall until the movie started.

So, we headed out, and just as we were about to start walking in the mall, he saw someone he knew and immediately stopped to engage. We introduced ourselves, and they proceeded to chat, catching up on old times.

It was fine at first, but then when I saw that they were old friends, I decided to excuse myself and give them time to chat, so I eased away.

They just kept talking, never even knowing I had left, because I looked back in case, I needed to indicate to him that I was moving on down the mall. They never looked my way, so I rolled away, not that far at all. I wanted to window shop.

However, like I said, it was crowded, so the crowd must have swallowed me up, and I couldn't see them, and I was sure they couldn't see me.

I was about 50 yards away when I heard him calling for me. Theo, Theo, Theo in this frantic voice.

It actually alarmed me. I thought something was wrong. I turned around and in the crowd of people I saw him pushing people aside to get to me.

When he finally saw me, he ran up to me and said, " Why didn't you tell me you were leaving. I got all worried. You can't do that kind of stuff!"

I could only look at him, stunned. Trying to figure out what had just happened and how things turned so quickly.

I immediately said, "Chill out. Everything is okay! Calm down." He was clearly upset with me. But then he repeated it, "Don't do that, man!"

Things shifted in my mind right then. He wasn't looking at me as a fellow businessman, friend, or even a fellow grown ass man!

He was looking at me as if I were a child. In this instance, a child had wandered off in a big mall without checking with his parents.

Someone he had to watch over and protect. After all, I was disabled.

I had not checked with him before I wandered off. How could I do something like that? And he wasn't going to tolerate it anymore.

We went in and watched the movie, but I never invited him out again.

I never saw him the same after that experience.

You see, I was looking for a friend, and he wanted to be a caregiver. I had enough caregivers already! I paid for that service.

Chapter 4: I Can't See It, but I have Faith

One of my most life-changing moments happened during the process of iron sharpening iron.

The pastor liked meeting for breakfast one-on-one with his core group of men.

At one of these meetings, he asked me what one of the most important things I wanted to accomplish now that God had restored what the cankerworm had destroyed (I will explain this further in a later chapter). Now that my wife and I were back together.

I didn't need to think about it. I immediately said, I want to have a child, but I didn't think I could because of my spinal cord injury.

He immediately asked questions that I really couldn't answer.

He challenged me to try and told me God has already gotten us back for a reason.

I could tell he didn't fully understand how a paralyzed man could have a child, but Pastor always had faith.

We prayed right there in the restaurant over eggs and bacon.

That night, I shared with my wife that we should just start trying.

I even made plans to get checked out but never made it to the specialist.

A few weeks later, my wife came home with the good news. She was pregnant.

We had Theo Jr. in May of 1998.

Pastor still finds humor in saying he didn't know how a paralyzed man was going to have a baby.

News flash to all of you! Not everything is paralyzed on a paralyzed man!

Chapter 5: My Experiences as Coach

I shared with you in my first life how my football coach impacted my life. I loved that time as a young athlete with my coach.

I never dreamed I would have an opportunity to be one. I coached both of my kids, but I want to share a little about how I came to coach my daughter's softball team.

Like any parent, we encourage our kids to play sports. I tried all the sports with my daughter, trying to figure out what she wanted to play.

My son was easy. We can discuss him later, but my daughter, Kimmi, was different.

I called her Kim Possible, after a children's cable TV show by the same name, because I believed anything was possible for her. She has that spark.

We tried field hockey. We tried cross-country running. We tried basketball. Kickball, too much running, she said.

Finally, she took a little liking to softball, so she tried out and wanted to play, but she wasn't very good at it. The other girls who played with travel teams were much better.

She was embarrassed but still liked it.

I even remember one of the travel team coaches coming up to me and encouraging me not to come back, but to try something else.

Honestly, I was offended. We were the only black father and daughter there, and it felt like they didn't want us there.

I recall discussing it with my daughter. I asked her if she really wanted to play. "Yes, Dad."

"You will need to work hard at it, but if you do, I guarantee you that you can be better than any of the girls who laughed at you." She said okay, and that is what motivated us.

I provided her with all the right equipment and training videos, and we practice regularly. I couldn't do everything due to my physical condition, but I made up for it with verbal instructions.

I purchased her training sessions with trainers to do what I couldn't. She became very good at it.

She started playing on another travel team, not the one that didn't want the black father and daughter who told me to try another team.

This travel team saw her potential. This travel team even saw my potential. The head coach, Leo Brown, asked me to be his assistant coach as well.

That's how I became a coach. I enjoyed coaching with Coach Brown. He too saw Theo, not disabled Theo.

I had a wonderful time. Didn't ever believe I could do it, but again, that head coach saw beyond my wheelchair and saw determination.

We were a great travel team! Kim Possible was great, too. I purchased her a special bat with Kim Possible written on it, so that she knew I believed in her.

With that bat at hand one day playing in Upper Dauphin, I was sitting watching them play against another travel team.

Kimmi was coming up to bat. I went quickly to get something out of the van, thinking I had time. All of a sudden, I heard the crowd roar. I turned around and came back only to see my daughter, who other girls had laughed at, coming into home plate.

She had just hit a grand slam home run. I missed it.

Can you believe it? All I saw was her coming into the home plate with her teammates surrounding her, cheering for her.

I never told her I missed it.

She had others throughout her playing days. I didn't miss those.

And by the way. Those girls who laughed at her. I know for a fact that two of them were on the same team when my daughter, Kim Possible made the Central Dauphin High School Softball Team.

Kimmi, stop playing high school softball her senior year.

She never told me why, but I suspected she was being harassed by the other white players on her team. She was the only black player on the Central Dauphin High School Softball team at that time.

Chapter 6: Can I Have Fries with that?

Can inspiration be a bad thing? Sure, it can. But maybe not always. Let me explain what I mean, especially when it comes to people with disabilities.

You see, people with disabilities are often viewed as "inspirations" by people without disabilities, not for climbing a mountain or curing cancer, but for simply living our lives.

Going to work. Buying groceries. Picking up our kids. Doing everyday things that everybody does.

Now, you would think that being called "inspirational" would always feel good, right? I mean, who doesn't want to inspire others? But for many of us, me included, it doesn't feel that way at all.

Let me tell you another story that explains why. One of the greatest joys of my life has been teaching my kids how to play sports. I shared this already.

My daughter played softball, and my son plays basketball, and let me tell you, he turned out pretty good. Real good. Fast forward a little, he went on to play college ball and now semi-pro.

However, this happened during junior high. One night after practice, we were both tired and hungry, so we pulled into a Wendy's drive-thru, our little father-and-son tradition.

I placed our order at the first window and rolled up to the second. That's when I remembered my fries.

So, as I handed the woman my card, I said, "Can I have fries with that?"

She smiled politely. My son came up to the window to grab the food. And then I saw that look. I have seen it many times over my life. Her head tilted slightly. Her eyes softened like she was about to cry.

And then she said it, that wordless sigh we all know too well: "Aaaaah."

She looked at me and said I inspired her. I smiled because that's what we do. I knew I had to take that hit.

I took the bag, thanked her, and drove off.

But as we pulled away, I felt lousy. I couldn't shake that feeling. I wanted to tell my son,

"I'm more than what that woman just saw. I'm more than my wheelchair. I'm more than someone's feel-good moment."

That young lady at Wendy's didn't mean any harm. She did what so many people without disabilities do. She saw my existence as inspiration.

But here's the thing:

Not every person with a disability should be your source of inspiration just because we exist, or because we do the same ordinary things you do.

If you think about it, what she found "inspiring" wasn't that I had overcome something, it was that I was a dad in a wheelchair buying his son a burger and fries.

That's it! An everyday thing. But when a person with a disability does it, suddenly it's seen as heroic, it's extraordinary, something to marvel at.

That kind of inspiration isn't based on respect. It's based on pity. And pity has never empowered anyone.

We see this all the time. In commercials, on posters, in those "heartwarming" social media videos:

A kid with Down syndrome kicking a soccer ball.

A man using a prosthetic leg running a race.

A woman using a wheelchair going to work.

And the caption always reads something like, "What's your excuse?"

Let me say this clearly:

People with disabilities should not exist to make other people feel better about themselves.

Now, if you know me, if you know my story, if you know what I've built and fought for, and that inspires you? Then fine. I'll take that. That's earned inspiration. That's real.

But if you have never met me. If you don't know my story, then what inspires you? Me, ordering fries at Wendy's or teaching my son to shoot a basketball? Then you're missing the point.

I am so much more than my disability. We all are.

So, if you really want to be inspired by me, get to know my story. Keep reading this book.

Know what I have overcome, what I have built, and what I continue to fight for.

Then, maybe, you'll see the real me.

And I promise. That story's worth being inspired by.

Chapter 7: The Unexpected Guest

Here is another short, but interesting story regarding my son Theo Jr. and a childhood friend.

They were teenager at this point.

It was a typical night. The whole family had gathered into bed. It was around midnight. All of a sudden, the doorbell begins to repeatedly ring. My son answered the door.

After hearing a voice, I realized it was someone he knew. One of his friends, so my son came to our room saying who it was and that his friend was scared and panic. That he ran from home because he was being beaten by his parent.

He then asked could his friend just stay until the next day. This was on a Friday night. The friend insisted he was afraid to go back, and my son pleaded with me.

Since he was safe and unharmed and I knew he lived nearby from other visits, I agreed telling them I would straighten it all out in the morning.

Morning came and I chatted with his friend, explaining why he shouldn't be running away from home. After the talk, I said let me take you home and I did.

I watch as my son went with him to the door. I instructed him to explain. The parent and I had seen each other before at games, so she gave me a thumbs up and my son and I left.

The talk must have worked. He never came over again in panic.

I tell this story because the kid happened to be Micah Parsons, who went on to play football with Penn State, drafted in the first round in 2021 by the Dallas Cowboys and currently plays for the Green Bay Packers.

Chapter 8: There He Goes

Here's another story with my son, Theo Jr.

He was playing college basketball by this time. He had a game in Philadelphia at Harcum University.

I couldn't go to all his games, so when the team played close, I tried to make it. Philly is about two hours away. Two hours for me from Harrisburg. I drive slowly.

I had promised my son I would be there. He was starting that game, not coming off the bench, so he wanted me there, and I wanted to be there.

Typically, games start around 7:00 p.m., so I left early. I didn't know where I was going, and I was driving alone. Yes, we do that sometimes. Go places by ourselves. It's the greatest feeling ever, not needing someone all the time.

Anyway, I thought I had arrived in plenty of time. But it turned out to be one of the most difficult colleges to find that I've ever experienced.

By now, it was dark and starting to rain, which made navigating even worse. I finally located the gym where they were playing. I saw people gathering to go in, so I followed.

There was a line, so I waited. The only time I use my disability card is at movies or concerts, those are the rare times I'll take that little privilege to skip the line. It's one of those pity perks non-disabled folks bestow on us, "the going to the front of the line" thing.

But not this time. I waited.

I could hear the players warming up. I couldn't wait for my son to see me roll in, to see his smile, knowing I kept my word. I always tell him keeping your word is important.

Finally, it was my turn, to pay for my ticket.

Just as the ticket taker was about to hand it to me, I noticed out of the corner of my eye that the attendees were going downstairs.

So, I asked, "Where's the accessible entrance?"

He gave me this puzzled look, clearly running things through his mind. Then he said something that shocked me:

"There isn't any. Now that I think about it, all three entrances have steps."

I said, "You've got to be wrong. This is a university!"

He quickly said, "hold on," and went to talk to a security guard.

He came back, but by then the crowd behind me was getting restless, folks wanted to get inside.

He looked at me and said, "I was right. There are no accessible entrances."

I said, "My son is playing tonight. I just drove two hours to get here. There's got to be a way."

By then, people were walking past me, heading down the stairs, students, staff, whoever. I moved aside so others could buy their tickets but kept talking to the man.

A few people looked concerned, but not enough to stop and help.

The buzzer sounded, the game had started. And that's when it hit me: I wasn't getting in.

My son didn't even know I was outside fighting to get through the door.

Finally, I put my advocate hat on. I said firmly,

"I need the contact information for the president of this university. What's his name?"

And this is what he said:

"The president was just here in line listening. There he goes, going down the stairs. He walked right past you."

I turned just in time to see the back of his head before he disappeared down those steps.

I went completely silent. I didn't say another word. I knew exactly what I was dealing with.

I turned around and drove home.

On the drive, I called my attorney. It wasn't about me anymore. I needed to make sure this never happened again to another wheelchair user and I did.

That night, I told my son that I had kept my word to him, that I did show up. I explained what happened. He understood, but he was clearly disappointed.

He had played a great game that night.

I just wasn't allowed to see it.

Chapter 9: Woody's

One of the most enjoyable times in my life was my time at Woody's gym, a membership fitness center back when gyms were booming everywhere.

I have always enjoyed working out. Even back in my undergraduate college days, I was good at figuring out my own exercise routines, how to strength train and still get some cardio in.

But Woody's was different. I loved that place.

It reminded me of the old TV show Cheers, "where everybody knows your name."

That was Woody's, except instead of a bar, it was a gym. I would roll in, and before I could even check in, the staff would yell out,

"Theo!" Not Norm! Like on the show, but close enough. (If you've ever watched Cheers, you get the reference.)

I was, once again, a "first." Not the first Black member this time, but the first wheelchair user, the first quadriplegic, to ever join that mainstream fitness center.

I never set out to be a first at anything. I was just determined not to let anything stop me from doing what I enjoyed.

And that's exactly what Woody's gave me, a place where I wasn't seen as "different." I was just Theo.

I made some great friends there. People I still talk to today. Two of them, Ed and Nora Proctor, were trainers and staff at Woody's. They later went on to open a bakery in Midtown called Ed & Nora's Bakery, tucked inside a little Mid-Town bookstore.

Every time I pass by the gym's spot, I can't help but smile. It reminds me of those days at Woody's, the laughter, the sweat, the feeling of belonging.

Maybe too comfortable. I never told anyone this but one time I completely forgot and left my 5-year-old son there playing in the nursery, I was almost home when I remembered I had taken him with me. He was fine, still playing, never knowing I forgot about him.

Chapter 10: The Great Escape

I had just pulled up from work. I usually went to Woody's right after work, because if I ever went home first, that workout wasn't happening. So, straight to the gym it was.

But this particular day, I was tired. Worn out.

There was a Dunkin' Donuts right up from Woody's on Paxton Street, you had to cross a busy, two-way road with traffic flying by. On the other side of Dunkin' sat a nursing home called Spring Creek.

So, I parked at Woody's, hopped out of my van, and decided to roll in my wheelchair across the street to grab a cup of coffee. Probably a donut too, let's be real, I was addicted to those donuts.

As I started crossing Paxton, weaving carefully between the traffic, I noticed a woman standing on the opposite sidewalk in a nursing uniform. She was staring at me hard.

At first, I thought maybe she recognized me. I know a lot of people, so I waved and kept rolling. I was on a mission for that donut.

Then, out of nowhere, I heard this loud voice, really loud, cutting right through the traffic noise.

She yelled, "You can't be out here! You need to come with me right now!"

Before I could react, she literally started stopping traffic, and came across to me, arms waving and trying to guide me toward the nursing home across the street.

I shouted back,

"Lady, I'm not a resident of that nursing home! I'm coming from Woody's!"

She looked at Woody's. Then she looked back at me. I could see the realization wash over her face. She had just mistaken me as someone escaping from the nursing home.

And that's when I just lost it. I started laughing hard.

All I could say was, "I just wanted a donut!"

She started apologizing over and over again, then darted back across the street, dodging cars as she went.

I went inside, got my coffee and two donuts that day. I figured I earned them.

Chapter 11: There's No Place Like Home

The family got a little bigger. It was Roe and me, along with Kimmi and Theo Jr.

We needed a bigger house. Roe had her house, and I had mine, both too small for all of us. So, we decided it was time to find something new together.

Our pastor, Dr. Ashe, always said, "We have everything in the house." Meaning, whatever you need, someone in the church can probably help. We always tried to support our church family first, so that's where we started.

Sure enough, one of our members, Vicky, was a realtor who had helped several families in the congregation buy homes. She gladly offered to help us too.

Now, here's the big issue and she admitted it right up front there weren't any homes that were truly wheelchair accessible. So, we settled on looking for a ranch-style home, and I told her I could handle any additional modifications myself.

Even that wasn't easy. It had to be a ranch on flat land, no hills, no steep driveways. I wanted this home to be my dream house. Not fancy, just fully livable and free of barriers. After years of hard work, I felt like I had earned that. I wanted a home where I could come and go without asking anyone to open a door or lend a hand.

Roe agreed, and she took on the major task of working with Vicky to narrow down options. I couldn't go into most of the homes they toured, even the ranches because they weren't accessible. So, I had to trust her to find what would work best for us.

Whenever one looked promising, she would take pictures of the inside while I waited in the van. Some houses she visited on her own. We did this for months, and it started wearing us down financially. We were still paying the mortgage on her house too.

Then finally, a break. Roe found one.

It was a ranch with an oversized two-car garage, a long double-wide driveway, and the whole neighborhood was flat. That was a win right there.

Now, if only the inside was workable. Roe said it was great, and the pictures looked promising too. She told me it was "bigger on the inside than it looked on the outside." I later found out that was definitely true.

So, without seeing the interior myself, I trusted her judgment and said, "Let's do it." For whatever reason, the sellers liked us and accepted our offer even over others.

We didn't expect things to move so fast. Suddenly, we had to sell both of our old houses. Renting them out wasn't an option. We had tried that with her house before, and it was a nightmare.

Before moving in, a contractor friend of mine built a temporary wooden ramp in the back so I could finally go inside. And when I did, it took my breath away. It was beautiful, and yes, much bigger on the inside.

Once we settled, I went to work designing the accessible features I had always dreamed of.

We added a large, fully accessible shower off the master bedroom. Roe had her bathroom on one side, and I had my new bathroom on the other, complete with an automatic door that opened to a newly built double wide patio. The patio had a permanent concrete ramp with railings, and I even put an automatic skylight that opened for fresh air in the newly built bathroom area.

From the back patio another automatic door led into the main family room.

But I didn't stop there. I installed a self-operating stair lift that went down to a massive unfinished basement. It ran the entire width and length of the house.

We had the basement fully renovated into another family/game room, a separate fitness room, and my private office. The floors were laminated, the ceiling was dropped with recessed lighting, and my office had a push-button lock and a built-in marble-top desk. It was perfect, exactly how I envisioned it.

I handled the accessibility, and Roe handled the decorating. Together, we made it a home.

And here's what most non-disabled people may never fully understand: this was the first home in my entire life where I could come and go freely. No asking someone to open a door. No waiting for help. Just independence, built right into the entire home.

With smart home devices, I could control lights, doors, and everything else without needing help.

We lived there for 25 years. My kids grew up there. My favorite aunt passed away there. I tended a garden in the backyard, planting and pruning every flower myself.

I taught Kimmi how to swing a softball bat and Theo Jr. how to throw a baseball and later, how to shoot a basketball there. I even installed a camera with night lights so I could watch him and his friends play ball in the driveway after dark.

Now, you might ask. Why sell a perfect home like that?

Well, there were a few reasons. First, the yard was just too big. Too much upkeep. It got harder and harder to "keep up with the Joneses."

Then there were the constant repairs. Something always needed fixing or replacing, and finding reliable people got harder. Too many tried to take advantage.

But the final contributor came with a backstory.

See, Roe became a bit of a "fix-it" person. I blame those DIY shows she was hooked on. She was always painting, redecorating, or "improving" something. It always looked good, but sometimes it went wrong.

One day she decided to repaint the kitchen. She pulled the refrigerator out to get behind it with good intention, right? But when she pushed it back, she unknowingly bent the copper water line. A slow leak began that nobody knew about.

That night, we went to Bible study, came home late, and went straight to bed.

The next morning, my son came upstairs and said, "Dad, there's water in the basement." He said it so casually, I figured it was a small puddle.

Since my attendant hadn't arrived yet, I couldn't get up. Roe went down to check and came rushing back in a panic. "It's flooded! There's a lot of water!"

I called a close friend who lived nearby. He came right over, shut off the water, and assessed the damage.

The entire basement, my office, fitness room, furniture, ceiling, flooring, all waterlogged and ruined.

Insurance covered the repairs, but something inside me shifted. The house didn't feel the same anymore.

When we decided to sell, we didn't want just anyone buying it. We waited for someone who would appreciate the accessible features.

And we found her; a woman whose father used a wheelchair and needed a home just like ours. She fell in love with it immediately.

That's when we knew. It was time to let it go. We moved on.

Chapter 12: A Few Thoughts on Community Leadership

If you ask any of my closest colleagues to describe one of my best qualities, many of them would likely say this: Theo is a visionary, a servant leader.

I never named that within myself during my early years. It wasn't until my third life that I began to see it clearly. I realized I had a gift for seeking new opportunities, ideas, and initiatives, standing at the forefront of the planning stage, guiding them through implementation, and then moving on to the next vision.

If I had been a man of great wealth, I would never have been bored. But instead, I learned to carry my visions forward with faith, determination, and persistence, often with little more than belief to hold them up.

One of the guiding sayings I have repeated often came from my pastor, Dr. Clifford Ashe:

"People with vision don't have money. People with money don't have vision."

That truth stayed with me and shaped my perspective on leadership and the work I was called to do.

I've always had vision but never enough money. Here is an example.

Chapter 13: Live Well Fitness Center

Like I said earlier, I've always enjoyed working out. Staying active has always been part of my life, but finding a fitness center that actually had people with disabilities in mind. That was always the challenge.

As much as I loved being at Woody's, it was never really designed for me. I had to figure out my own ways to use equipment that wasn't accessible. If something didn't fit, I improvised.

Eventually, I started working with a personal trainer to get even more out of my workouts. One of my staff at my agency also happened to be a fitness trainer.

His name was **Jesse Swoyer**.

One day, Jesse and I were at Platinum Fitness. He was stretching me out, doing my range-of-motion exercises, when I noticed a machine across the room. I looked at it for a while and said quietly, "If they just made one simple change to that equipment, I could use it."

We talked about it for a bit, then went back to our workout. I didn't think much more of it.

A few days later, at our next session, Jesse brought it up again. He said, "Theo, I did some research." He pulled out a picture of something called an ADA Trainer, a workout station designed specifically for people with disabilities, but that could be used by anyone.

Jesse's eyes lit up as he said, "We should convince Platinum to buy one."

I didn't even hesitate. I told him flat out, "They're not going to do that. People with disabilities aren't their target audience." At that time, fitness centers were all about the "perfect body" image, six-packs, mirrors, and muscle shows. Inclusion wasn't part of the plan.

Then it hit me. I said, "Why don't we do it? My agency should open a fitness center, one built from the ground up for people with disabilities, with accessible equipment like this ADA Trainer."

I had the vision. What I didn't have was the money. And I wasn't sure if my board would see what I saw.

Still, I put together a proposal and presented it to them. To my surprise, they didn't just support it, they embraced it.

One of my favorite board members, **David Reager, Esq.**, who served with my agency for 31 years and has since passed away, stood up in that meeting and said, "I'll donate $20,000 to purchase the ADA Trainer."

I'll never forget that moment. David always believed in me, always supported my ideas. **Thank you, David.**

And **thank you, Jesse**. You believed in the vision, too. Jessie went on to become the first Director of the Live Well Fitness Center, running it for years before starting his own fitness business.

If you ever need a fitness guru who truly understands people of all abilities, check out Jesse's work at jesseswoyer.com. He's the real deal.

Chapter 14: Community Leader

One of my favorite authors is John Maxwell, who has written countless books on leadership. I absorbed his teachings and combined them with my own lived experiences, and from that mix, my unique perspective on leadership was born.

Here's one perspective I hold on to: leadership can be taught, but it can also be caught.

There are leaders who have taught me valuable lessons outright, and there are others I simply observed, catching wisdom from the way they moved, made decisions, and carried themselves.

I shared earlier in my first life about the OVR counselor who told me I wasn't college material when I said I wanted to go to college.

He shut that door on me with a single sentence. If not for seeing my friend leave early one morning and asking where she was headed, I might never have pursued higher education at all.

That moment wasn't taught; it was caught.

The truth is, you can learn a lot from others, but without those moments of catching something, a glimpse of possibility, sparks of courage, and examples of resilience, you may never gain the full benefit of what leadership really means.

The following few chapters will share stories of the leaders who shaped me. Some I learned from directly. Others, I simply caught the lessons they left in their wake.

Each one left an imprint on my third life, the life of a visionary, servant leader, and advocate.

Theo-ism: *Leadership isn't just taught in books or classrooms. Much of it is caught through lived experience and watching others.*

Chapter 15: Here's the Keys

In early 1989, I landed my job fairly quickly after graduating with my master's degree from Temple University.

I was hired as the Public Affairs Director for the Mental Health Association of Cumberland, Dauphin, and Perry Counties. The Executive Director was John Clendian. He was a nice older gentleman.

It was a good job, actually, my first professional job, and I was excited just to be working and earning a paycheck.

The salary was only $16,000 a year, but I knew I could do better.

Until another opportunity came along, it felt good to know I was making a difference in the mental health field.

Most of my work involved advocacy, helping people who were involuntarily committed to mental health institutions and wanted to be released if they felt their rights were being violated.

While doing this job, I was living with my college girlfriend, Roe, from my women's history class. She was teaching, and I was underemployed, but we were doing well.

One day, I was meeting with my attendant care case manager, who visited on a monthly basis at the time. She had to ask those required questions, like whether I was happy or depressed.

You know the kind, the silly questions they asked people with disabilities because they assumed we were all unhappy living with disabilities, so they needed to "protect" us.

Anyway, that's another topic.

She casually mentioned that she was part of a coalition working on what she called a "huge initiative." She said, "You should come and volunteer to assist us since you're a social worker."

She went on to tell me that a group had formed to write a proposal to establish a Center for Independent Living. She explained what a Center for Independent Living was and why it was important to establish one in our area, as it was a federally funded initiative.

She gave me the number of the coalition leader, whose name was Marsha Grim.

My case manager left, but she definitely had my attention.

I eventually called Marsha and started attending the planning meetings. It was fascinating, and I quickly got involved.

Long story short, the coalition made up of community leaders from different agencies pulled together an outstanding grant proposal and submitted it to the Department of Education.

To my surprise, it was awarded to us and at the highest amount ever awarded: $199,000.

Everyone was excited, especially Marsha, who was now the President of this grassroots coalition.

Marsha was also leading the hiring process for the Executive Director position, and she knew I had just graduated with my master's degree. She asked if I was interested in being interviewed.

It blew me away. I knew very little about running an organization as an Executive Director, even less about Centers for Independent Living. I had only just learned what they were through my case manager.

Not only that, but I had just started my position as Public Affairs Director. It had only been six months.

I had grown fond of John as a boss, and I couldn't imagine telling him I might leave, but I also couldn't ignore the opportunity.

I had a real dilemma. I told Marsha I would think about it.

It didn't take long. The next day, I called her and said yes, I would love an interview.

I never found out how many people were interviewed, but it was a national competition.

I was hired unanimously!

Leaving John was hard. I could tell he was disappointed, but given the choice, who wouldn't take that kind of career move.

To this day, my next steps make me wonder how divinely everything worked out.

Marsha met with me at the new office.

She had rented the third floor of a newly renovated building for the new Center, which we named The Center for Independent Living of Central PA (CILCP) Let me fast forward really quickly. This same center is now renamed to Thrive, and the CEO is Brittany Boyd-Chisholm, who I first hired at age 18 when I was CEO of CILCP over 36 years ago.

Back to the story. I share this often. We were both wheelchair users. Marsha had multiple sclerosis, and I, as you know, am a quadriplegic.

We sat there side by side, looking at the empty offices: five offices and a large conference room, all vacant.

She looked at me, handed me a set of keys, and said these words: "Start a Center."

I said, "I got you."

Thank you, Marsha, for believing in me.

From that point on, I had a mission. It began with getting some staff.

The grant called for six positions: an Executive Director (which I filled), an Office Manager, two Independent Living Specialists, a Peer Mentor, and an Information and Referral Specialist.

I hired great staff but will only highlight two that truly stood out during that time. Margo Wright was the first person I hired as Office Manager. We grew to be like brother and sister. She was always there for me, good or bad. Margo became Director of Attendant Care. **Thank you, Margo.**

I also hired Janetta Green as an Independent Living Specialist. She stayed with me right up to my retirement, always dependable. Always standing in the gap. She allowed me to operate in my strength, by handling the day-to-day stuff. I was the visionary, the face. Janetta became my Director of Operations. When I retired, Janetta became CEO. **Thank you, Janetta.**

The biggest concern was learning everything I could about what a Center for Independent Living really was.

I started researching. Back then, we didn't have the modern internet. We had AOL and the early World Wide Web. But I managed to find a documentary on Ed Roberts, a 60 Minute special.

I watched it over and over again. The words Ed spoke mirrored my life since the day of that life-changing tackle on the football field on April Fool's Day.

I called Ed on the phone after many tries to find him.

We talked. I told him my story, told him I had just been funded, and asked if he would come to help me.

He agreed, to my surprise.

I flew him and his personal attendant in, and he stayed for two weeks.

During that time, we talked about everything. I was a sponge.

Everyone wanted to meet Ed. All the folks from that original coalition couldn't believe he was here in PA. We had a lot of news coverage.

Ed and I even co-facilitated a conference during that time called "Becoming Your Own Best Advocate."

It was another thrilling, life-changing moment for me.

Theo-ism: *Vision without goals is fantasy. Goals without vision become drudgery. But when you have both, you have a mission.*

Chapter 16: Justin Dart — "Lead On. I Love You!"

Not long after meeting Ed Roberts, I had the honor of meeting another legend, Justin Dart, often referred to as the Father of the ADA.

Pennsylvania was hosting its first Independent Living Conference, and I was part of the planning committee. I even came up with the theme: "Power Through Knowledge."

We invited Justin Dart to be the keynote speaker.

To me, this was another opportunity to soak up wisdom.

By then, I already had book knowledge. I had spent nearly eight years in school, from community college to Edinboro University for my bachelor's degree and finally earned my master's degree in social work from Temple University.

But the Independent Living Movement was something new. I was still learning the deeper meaning of independent living and understanding just how essential Centers for Independent Living were within this national network.

The gentle power of Justin Dart. Justin carried himself with a quiet strength. He had the love of America behind him, and you could feel it in the room.

He was a gentle spirit, kind, thoughtful, humble, yet his presence demanded attention.

I'll admit it: I was intimidated. Maybe even more so than when I met Ed Roberts.

There was an aura about Justin. It's hard to describe, but when you were near him, you knew you were standing in the presence of greatness.

What I took away most from Justin Dart was this lesson:

"Be quiet in spirit, but when it's time to speak, speak boldly, with courage."

That one truth stayed with me. It shaped how I led, how I advocated, and how I approached every conversation from that day forward.

It helped form the foundation of my leadership and my voice within the Independent Living Movement.

Chapter 17: Maggie Shreve — The Architect of Independent Living Standards

Not long after, I met Maggie Shreve, another powerhouse in the Independent Living world. Everyone talked about Maggie and her consulting work for CILs across the country. I knew I had to bring her in too, and I'm so glad I did.

Maggie taught me the core components of Independent Living, the standards, assurances, and the key indicators of what makes a true Center.

She emphasized that the mission must always remain clear and that no matter what, we must never stray from it.

I never did.

Her lessons became part of the DNA of the Center for Independent Living of Central PA.

Theo-ism: *You don't know what you don't know, and the more you know, the more you should realize how much more there is to know.*

Chapter 18: Christina Forbrich — The Standard of Excellence

Another influential person in my early days was Christina Forbrich, who worked with the Office of Vocational Grant Management.

Christina was instrumental in guiding us through the technical requirements of our federal grant application, which received a perfect score and the highest award amount ever at the time: $199,000.

That had never happened before.

Christina taught me about the commitment to excellence.

She made it clear that if you say in your proposal that you're going to do something, you do it.

If you promise a deliverable, you deliver.

That level of integrity builds trust and opens doors for future grants and partnerships.

I carried that principle with me throughout my entire career.

Chapter 19: The Late Mayor Stephen Reed — From Adversary to Ally

Then there was Mayor Stephen Reed, the longtime Mayor of Harrisburg.

Our relationship started as pure adversaries but eventually grew into mutual respect.

In the early days, Mayor Reed and I didn't get along. I wanted Harrisburg to become a model city for accessibility, a city where people with disabilities could live, work, and move freely.

But time and time again, the city made decisions that excluded us.

He probably thought I would back down. He learned quickly that I wouldn't.

I had learned from the best: Ed Roberts, Justin Dart, and others, and I understood that access wasn't a privilege. It was a right.

If people without disabilities could access a product, service, or public space, then people with disabilities should have that same right.

That included buses, taxis, and curb cuts.

At one point, Mayor Reed even tried to place a moratorium on issuing disability parking placards, claiming there was abuse of the system.

But I knew better. It was really about wanting to generate more parking revenue.

We went back and forth in the newspapers for weeks, a public battle of wills.

But in the end, something remarkable happened.

Years later, the same Mayor Reed who once fought me tooth and nail presented me with a proclamation, recognizing my leadership and our work in making Harrisburg a city that included all citizens, especially those with disabilities.

Theo-ism: *The loudest voice doesn't always lead the change!*

Chapter 20: The First Marriage

I saw her across the room.

She caught my eye immediately.

She was beautiful, with a small black mole on her forehead, just noticeable enough to make her stand out from any girl I had ever seen.

It was my first time seeing Rovenia "Roe" Whaley. We were both in a Women's History course. I'll be honest, I only took that class because I needed something light. The rest of my schedule that semester was packed with tough classes.

But after seeing her, that class became the highlight of my week.

I kept watching her, trying to be discreet, though I probably failed miserably. Every now and then, she caught me staring. I'm sure she thought I was a creep.

And here's the truth: I never said a single word to her that entire semester. Not one.

After staring that much, I didn't have the nerve to start a conversation. So, she remained the girl who lived rent-free in my mind.

Then, as fate would have it, our paths crossed again in the most unexpected way.

One day, she showed up in my college dorm and was introduced as a new attendant hired by the Office of Disabled Student Services (ODSS).

I was living in Shaffer Hall, where all the students with disabilities were housed. ODSS hired non-disabled students as attendants to help us with our daily living routines, things like getting in and out of bed, dressing, or reaching things we couldn't.

And now, the girl I had secretly admired for an entire semester was assigned to assist me.

So, yes, the woman of my dreams would now be helping me get dressed and undressed.

I was a lucky man!

And obviously, because this is my story, she was overwhelmed by my rugged manly body parts, and the rest is history.

That's my story, and I'm sticking to it.

We dated for about a year. I graduated, while she stayed behind at Edinboro to finish her degree.

When I later graduated from Temple University, she moved to Harrisburg. We got a place together, two young professionals starting out, full of hope and ambition. She got a job as a special education teacher, and I was working as Public Affairs Director.

Things were good until they weren't.

Yelp, the ultimatum. You know the one:

"If we're not getting married, I need to move on."

I knew deep down I wasn't ready. But I also knew I couldn't stand the thought of losing her.

So, I did what many men in love do: I went along with it.

We got married at First Spirit Baptist Church in Edgemont.

And let me make something perfectly clear, I wasn't ready for marriage.

It was entirely my fault that our marriage ended in divorce just two years later.

But as the old saying goes: You don't miss the water until the well runs dry.

Chapter 21: The Breaking Point

I was just driving down the road. It was about a month after my divorce, and it was finally hitting me hard. You know that old saying, "you really don't know what you have until it's gone"? It's true.

I was hurting, really hurting, and missing my wife. I knew I had messed it all up. I wanted to be a better person. For the first time, I was realizing life wasn't necessarily about doing whatever it took to be "successful."

On paper, I had a great life. My career was thriving. I was still young, but already well-known in the community, a leader. I could afford to have a good time. So that wasn't it. Something deeper was missing.

Now that I had blown it with my wife, I kept wondering was she the missing piece? Did I just need her back? But I knew that wasn't going to happen. She had made that perfectly clear.

So, I kept driving. And then, out of nowhere, I started to cry. Hard. It was the feeling of being alone again, knowing I had messed up, and not knowing what to do next. It overwhelmed me.

I was experiencing great loss once again.

Up to that point, I had done everything society expected of a "real man."

I had overcome poverty.

I had survived a devastating accident that left me in a wheelchair.

I had worked hard, made it through undergraduate school, and then graduate school.

I had just turned 30 and was the CEO of my own agency.

And yet, here I was, driving down the road with tears streaming down my face. Something was wrong, really wrong, and I needed answers.

All that time, the radio had been playing, but I hadn't noticed. Then one thing cut through the noise: an announcement about a revival underway at the Harrisburg Forum. I knew the place.

People say this all the time, but it's real: a voice in my head said, "Go there right now."

I drove straight there, still crying. When I arrived, I couldn't remember how to get in. The front had steps, not an option.

But I remembered a back entrance with elevators and headed there, still with soggy eyes, on the verge of a full breakdown. Something was happening to me, and I wasn't in control anymore.

I made my way to the back and found the elevators. The place was strangely empty. Floor after floor, I searched. Each time I'd get off, follow the sound of music, push through doors, only to find a dead end. Five floors. Five tries.

Finally, I gave up. I decided to just go home. But as I was leaving, getting ready to press the elevator button, I saw another door.

And that same inner voice said, "Go through it."

I turned around. I pushed through. The music got louder. Another door. Then another. I opened it and started to see people. I was backstage.

Right then, the spirit started filling me again. I remembered that feeling from my early days, before the accident, when I used to go to church all the time. I had put all that behind me after my experience with the Elders praying over me, but now it was flooding back.

I sat backstage, listening to the speakers. No one said a word to me. There were folks back there coordinating the event, but maybe they thought I was a speaker waiting to go on.

After about twenty minutes, the preacher asked people to come forward for salvation and prayer.

And again, that voice asked me, "Why did you come here?"

I didn't answer. I just moved my wheelchair toward the stage, rolled around the curtain, and suddenly I was in front of the lights. The Forum was filled.

People were on their feet. A few had come up to the stage, including me. The preacher handed me the mic.

Right there, before hundreds of people, I confessed my sins. Tears rolled down my face. I could barely speak, but God understood.

Afterward, I went backstage and sat there, still crying. And when I looked up, there was my sister Annie. She hugged me. We cried together.

That night, I was a new man. It was a life-changing moment. One I have never told anyone about until now.

Chapter 22: The Immoveable Force

After my experience at the Forum, standing before hundreds of people and confessing my sins, I found myself constantly asking what God had in store for me next.

Remember the song, "Maybe God Is Tryin' To Tell You Somethin" by Shug Avery from The Color Purple?

That's exactly how I felt.

He was up to something.

I was changing.

One day, my niece Angie told me about a church she was attending. She was excited about a young preacher named Pastor Clifford Ashe. She urged me to visit.

And since I was learning to listen to that inner voice again, I went.

Not right away, of course. But eventually, I showed up to a Wednesday night Bible study, and I never stopped going after that first visit.

I know people say this often, but that night, it truly felt like Pastor Ashe was speaking directly to me.

It was as if someone had given him the "Cliff Notes" of my life (pun intended).

The church was called East Shore, and at that time, we held services at the Holiday Inn East.

From that first night on, I became a sponge. I didn't miss a single service, Wednesday or Sunday.

Under Pastor Ashe's teaching, I learned so much about God, about faith, and about myself. And over time, I realized something profound:

Pastor Ashe was my immovable force. We All Need One!

Men like me, men who are successful, confident, and think we've got it all figured out, need an immovable force.

Someone who refuses to be impressed by our excuses, our charm, or our so-called "wisdom."

Someone who won't tolerate our nonsense.

I had a lot of nonsense in me.

I remember one Sunday, after I had gotten in the habit of showing up to his office unannounced, Pastor Ashe looked up and said calmly, "You know I use this time to prepare for service."

That was his polite way of telling me to stop just dropping in.

I stopped showing up uninvited after that.

He did that sort of thing often, teaching me lessons without ever raising his voice. I was hardheaded, but he was even harder headed.

Under Pastor Ashe's leadership, I dedicated myself fully to serving God.

I settled on the fact that he was following God, and I needed to follow Pastor.

And very quickly, I discovered my ministry: serving the man God had placed in my life as my immovable force.

I served wherever I was needed.

Don't laugh, but I even joined the Men's Choir.

I will never forget singing on stage at Messiah College, sitting in my wheelchair alongside the other men. We actually sounded pretty good!

God truly works in mysterious ways.

That became even clearer the Sunday I looked up and saw my ex-wife walk into the sanctuary of East Shore.

I couldn't believe it.

I knew it wasn't because of me, especially since, just a few months earlier, she had made it very clear she never wanted to see me again.

Still, I got ahead of God and took it as a sign. Maybe she was softening. Maybe this was my second chance.

I was wrong.

I later learned that she almost stopped attending once she realized I was there.

Pastor told me years later that she had even asked him to keep me away from her.

One day, while driving, I broke down again, thinking about her, the marriage I had ruined, and the life I had lost.

I called Pastor.

"Pastor, this is Theo. You got a second to talk?"

"Of course," he said. "What's going on?"

"It's my ex-wife," I said. "She's coming to church now. You know her?"

He said, "Yes, we have talked. But she wants nothing to do with you. And, Theo, I need you to stop trying to talk to her."

"Pastor, I'm miserable without her," I said.

That's when my immovable force spoke words that would forever shape my faith:

"Theo, I'm going to tell you something, and I never want to have this conversation again until I bring it up.

You need to work on yourself.

Only God can restore what the cankerworm destroys (Joel 2:25).

You need to consider her dead."

I didn't fully understand it at the time.

But later, I did.

He wasn't being cruel. He was teaching me to surrender.

To stop chasing what God had already removed.

And if I truly believed the scripture that said God orders our steps and put in my life a Pastor after His own heart, then I had to accept that Pastor Ashe was part of that plan.

So, I obeyed.

I stopped trying to reach her.

I stopped asking questions.

And I started focusing on the Word of God.

After that conversation, I became a true disciple.

I studied the Word of God faithfully.

Pastor Ashe gathered a small group of men and made us his core group. We met daily at times, studying together, growing together, and being shaped into what he called the Mighty Men of Valor.

We even went to see The Lion King together and had a meeting afterward. I will never forget Pastor pulling a single line from the movie:

"You are more than what you have become."

He used that line to teach us that God was still molding us.

It stuck.

He often quoted 1 Samuel 22:2 to describe our group:

"All those who were in distress or in debt or discontented gathered around him [King David], and he became their commander. About four hundred men were with him."

We were Pastor Ashe's Mighty Men of Valor, once broken, discontented men, being trained and disciplined to become warriors for Christ.

We did everything together, and Pastor made sure I was included in everything.

He never saw my wheelchair as a limitation.

He often used me as an example to encourage the other men, though I admit, I didn't always like that. But I was determined to serve God's good shepherd.

We studied words like accountability, responsibility, reliability, integrity, and consistency.

Pastor taught us that these weren't just fancy words that rolled off the tongue; they were daily actions that we needed to live out every single day.

We read books on leadership.

Pastor introduced me to my favorite author, John Maxwell.

Once again, I became a sponge.

Eventually, I became a minister.

Our church grew and purchased land in Middletown. We built a multimillion-dollar facility and changed our name to DaySpring Ministries: The Dawning of a New Day.

At DaySpring, I served wherever Pastor needed me:

I led the Sick and Shut-In Ministry.

I coordinated and planned the Men's Breakfasts.

I directed the nonprofit arm of the church, first called Arms Around Harrisburg, later renamed Arms Around Communities as we expanded.

I was eventually appointed to the DaySpring Board of Directors.

The last major task I took on at DaySpring was helping coordinate Dr. Ashe's retirement.

Theo-ism: *Every strong man needs an immovable force, someone who tells him the truth, holds him accountable, and refuses to move until he grows.*

Chapter 23: The Second Marriage

I never wanted to have that conversation with Pastor Ashe again, so I kept my distance from my ex-wife while we both attended church. Of course, I kept an eye on her from afar, but I left her alone.

Then one day, God gave me a small glimpse, a gentle tap on the shoulder that whispered, "It's time. It's not over."

Out of the blue, one evening, my ex-wife called. Her voice was trembling; she was crying. Her mother, who lived in Pittsburgh, was showing signs of Alzheimer, and the neighbors said it was getting worse. She didn't know what to do. She was scared.

I did what I have always done best. Calmly make plans and execute them. I listened, calmed her down, and told her not to worry. We would figure it out. I told her to pack a few things and that I will drive her to Pittsburgh in the morning.

We made that trip together, with a friend along to help. When we arrived, it was clear that her mother couldn't stay there alone anymore. My ex-wife's apartment was too small for three people. Without thinking twice, I said, "She can stay with me. I have a two-bedroom house."

She looked at me, stunned.

In the days that followed, we packed up her mother's things and moved her to Harrisburg. That night, after everyone was settled, my ex-wife went home. I sat in the quiet and felt something I hadn't felt in a long time, hope.

A few days later, Pastor Ashe told me that she had come to him and asked if she could start dating me again. She called me her "Knight in Shining Armor."

So that's what we did. We started dating again. But this time was different. This time, my heart was in the right place.

A few weeks later, I rented a karaoke machine. I cooked dinner and told her I had a surprise waiting in the bedroom. When she walked in, the music started, R. Kelly's "If I Could Turn Back the Hands of Time."

As the lyrics played, "If I could turn, turn back the hands of time… then my darling, you'd still be mine".

I sang along, heart wide open.

When the song ended, I asked her to marry me again. Through her tears, she said, "Yes."

We remarried on a Wednesday night during Bible study.

Pastor Ashe officiated, and our church family surrounded us.

That was over thirty-three years ago. We've been together ever since. Two children, countless ups and downs, left turns when we should have gone right, but we never stopped climbing.

Chapter 24: Well-Intentional Folks

One morning, my wife was helping me get dressed when we noticed a swelling on the inside of my left groin. We both agreed I should see my doctor.

After some tests, the doctor said it was a cancerous tumor, but a mild one. He recommended surgery to remove it, and I went through with it. The operation went well, and we moved on with life, thankful it was behind us.

About a year later, it came back.

This time, the doctor called both of us into his office. I knew it was serious. Doctors don't ask for family meetings for nothing.

He sat across from us, looked me straight in the eye, and said, "It's malignant. The only way to stop it from spreading is to amputate your leg, all the way to the hip."

The words hit me like a freight train. I sat there, silent, trying to process it all. My heart was racing.

And then he said something that completely knocked me off balance.

He said, "It shouldn't be a big deal, you're paralyzed and don't use it anyway."

That sentence, that ableist statement, took my mind completely off the cancer. I left that office angry, hurt, and confused. For days, I wrestled with what he had said. I couldn't even think clearly about the surgery anymore.

It took conversations with my wife and Pastor Ashe to bring me back. They helped me see that my life, not my pride, was at stake.

I still think about that moment. I remember praying and reflecting on Christ in the Garden of Gethsemane when He said, "Not my will, but Your will be done." He asked God, "If this cup can pass from me, let it pass; nevertheless, not my will, but your will be done," but in the same breath, surrendered to God's plan. That moment hit me deeply.

I realized I didn't want to go through with it, but if this was something I had to face, I would trust God and go through it.

Once I wrapped my mind around that, I found peace in obedience, not because I wanted it, I didn't, but because I knew I wasn't walking alone.

So, I went through with the surgery. The doctors removed my leg, all the way to the hip socket. When I woke up in recovery, the doctor told me they got it just in time; the tumor had wrapped around a cluster of veins and was about to spread.

That one comment. That one ignorant remark could have cost me my life.

I don't believe the doctor meant any harm. He was well-intentional folk. But intention doesn't erase ignorance. His words were rooted in unconscious bias, the kind that devalues disabled lives without realizing it.

And that's why I tell this story.

Theo-ism: *Sometimes, the most dangerous harm doesn't come from hate; it comes from unexamined good intentions.*

Chapter 25: Out of the Blue

Two things have worked in my favor throughout my life, both worth passing on.

First, almost every blessing I have ever received, the kind that people call "success", came when I was busy helping someone else.

I wasn't chasing it. I wasn't even looking for it. It just showed up, out of the blue.

Second, I have always tried to keep learning and improving myself. I may not always know what's coming next, but I prepare for it anyway.

The more I learn, the more I realize how much I still don't know. And that curiosity keeps me ready for whatever's next.

Let me share a few examples.

Out of the blue, while I was deep in advocacy work, I got a call from Link Martin, an administrator at Temple University Harrisburg.

"Theo, I need an adjunct professor to teach two graduate courses. Your name came highly recommended. Would you consider it?"

I never dreamed of being a professor. I wasn't looking for it. I didn't even know where to begin,

but I was ready.

So, I said yes. I taught for years right up until I had to step away due to my cancer diagnosis.

I had the privilege of teaching some amazing graduate students, some of whom still reach out to me today.

Then, again, out of the blue, I got another call.

This time it was from Bill Gannon, Deputy Secretary, Office of Social Programs "Mr. Braddy, we need someone to fill a vacant seat on the Pennsylvania Human Relations Commission (PHRC). Your name has been recommended."

I hadn't applied for it, but once again, I answered the call.

I served as Commissioner for five years and had the honor of working alongside Homer Floyd, a civil rights legend who had marched and strategized with Dr. Martin Luther King Jr.

I also worked closely with Kabaa Brunson, another brilliant civil rights leader and Regional Director of PHRC.

When Homer retired, things changed. The Commission became more political. I had hoped Kabaa would succeed him. It would've been the right move, but politics had other plans.

I stayed on for a little while longer, but PHRC was never quite the same.

Still, life has a way of circling back in the most unexpected ways.

Years later, in 2023, I stood once again with Homer Floyd and Kabaa Brunson, this time not as colleagues in the trenches, but as brothers in legacy. Penn State University honored Homer and me with a Legacy Award for our lifetime contributions to civil rights and justice.

That night felt like a divine reminder, proof that the seeds you plant while helping others do grow, even if it takes decades to see them bloom.

And you know what? That wasn't the last "out of the blue" moment. They kept coming.

So, here is what I have learned: Just go about your business helping others. Keep learning. Keep preparing.

And watch how life will surprise you, with blessings that come... out of the blue.

Part IV – My Fourth Life: Legacy and Impact

Chapter 1: A Few Thoughts on Legacy and Impact

This part was the hardest to write about but could be the most impactful. You see, it involves the key figures in my fourth life. Some are folks with great influence. Some are just humble public officials who dedicated their lives to public service. All are individuals who honored me throughout this period of my life.

As I reflect on my year and a few months with the Biden Administration, I am struck by the immense respect and honor I received, being invited to sit at the table.

In Luke 14:7 11, it says:

7 When he [Jesus] noticed how the guests picked the places of honor at the table, he told them this parable:

8 "When someone invites you to a wedding feast, do not take the place of honor, for a person more distinguished than you may have been invited.

9 If so, the host who invited both of you will come and say to you, 'Give this person your seat.' Then, humiliated, you will have to take the least important place.

10 But when you are invited, take the lowest place, so that when your host comes, he will say to you, 'Friend, move up to a better place.' Then you will be honored in the presence of all the other guests.

11 For all those who exalt themselves will be humbled, and those who humble themselves will be exalted."

I have tried my best to live my life this way, never seeking a place of honor but often being invited as an honored guest. This was especially important during my time at the White House, where the disability voice needed to be heard.

I hope you enjoy this part of my fourth life!

Chapter 2: Riding Off into the Sunset

It had been almost 31 years, three decades as CEO of the Center for Independent Living of Central Pennsylvania.

Together, my staff and I built a legacy of change. We didn't just talk about advocacy; we lived it. I often told my team during staff meetings, "History will tell our story." And it will.

It was our Center that blocked Capital Transit from purchasing ten new buses that weren't accessible. The ADA had just been passed, and we were determined to ensure it mattered. We hit the streets, protested, and shut down the transfer station in downtown Harrisburg until they listened. The decision-makers finally agreed to order new buses with automatic lifts.

It was us who shut down City Council meetings until $200,000 was allocated for accessible curb cuts throughout the city.

It was us who launched a statewide transportation campaign that led to Pennsylvania's first paratransit legislation, creating a shared-ride program for people with disabilities, modeled after the one for senior citizens.

It was us who opened the first Live Well Fitness Center with accessible equipment designed for people with disabilities.

I could go on and on. Our fingerprints were everywhere.

I used to tell my staff, "If you ever doubt our impact, just look around." You can drive through our service area and see the evidence: the curb cuts, the ramps, the accessible businesses, and the lives that have changed.

If you searched the archives of The Patriot-News, you would find the stories, the protests, the victories, the battles with former Mayor Stephen R. Reed and the City Council.

At one point, the mayor and I were butting heads almost every week. I remember saying in one meeting, "Aren't people with disabilities citizens too?" It became one of my favorite quoted lines.

But after 31 years, I knew my time was coming to an end.

I have mentored a lot of young people with disabilities over the years. And one of the things I have always told them is this:

"When you get too comfortable, it's time for a change."

Because comfort can be dangerous, it can make you lazy. You stop creating. You stop pushing. You stop seeing new possibilities. You lose that drive, that lovin' feeling, that once made your work so powerful.

Oh yes, I would even make my staff laugh about it, quoting the Righteous Brothers: "You've lost that lovin' feelin', and it's gone, gone, gone." I used to play the song in staff meetings just to make the point stick.

And that's exactly what started happening to me. My job had become too easy. Too familiar. Too comfortable. So, I took my own advice. I needed to shake things up.

Our job, I told them, was to get that lovin' feeling back, to stay hungry, creative, and passionate.

But for me, after 31 years, I couldn't find it at the Center anymore.

At the age of 59, I decided to retire early.

Not because I was tired, but because I was ready for the next opportunity.

I started Theo Braddy Consulting, and just like that, I got that lovin' feeling back.

Even after retiring, my passion for helping others never stopped. Especially young people with disabilities who remind me of myself, hungry, hopeful, and sometimes a little lost.

Many of them come up to me and ask, "Theo, will you mentor me?"

I always say yes, but I give them a small test first. Something simple. Something that tells me if they're serious.

Usually, it's not the task that matters; it's whether they follow through. Accountability is everything.

More often than not, I find that some people aren't quite ready for that level of commitment. They want advice, but not accountability. And I get that I've been there too.

But for those who are serious, who show up and do the work, I go all in. Because I know what mentorship can do. Someone once believed in me when others didn't.

And that's the circle I'm trying to complete. To give back what was given to me.

Theo-ism: *When your work becomes too comfortable, it's the signal that it's time to grow again.*

Chapter 3: From Token to Trailblazer

One of the things that reignited my national leadership was an unpleasant experience with the Pennsylvania Statewide Independent Living Council, also known as the SILC.

I had been appointed to the SILC by three different governors over the years, so I had a long history with them. But this time it was different.

I had just retired after thirty-one years as CEO of the Center for Independent Living of Central PA, and I had no plans to return to council work. I wanted to focus on launching my consulting firm and finally enjoy some flexibility in my schedule.

Then came the call.

The executive director of the SILC reached out and told me how much the council "needed diversity." He said I could play an important role in helping them achieve that, even chair the recruitment committee.

I was hesitant, but I told him clearly: If I come back, I'm serious about diversity and inclusion, not symbolic gestures. He promised full support. A few weeks later, my appointment came through. It is important to point out that it happened pretty quickly.

Since my new consulting firm centered on diversity, equity, accessibility, and inclusion (DEAI), I didn't think it would be hard to find qualified candidates. I had established deep relationships throughout Pennsylvania with people who were familiar with my work and reputation. So, I started making calls.

I reached out to two Black attorneys I knew would bring strong, thoughtful leadership.

They agreed to be considered. I contacted colleagues from the Black, Indigenous, and People of Color (BIPOC) community and reconnected with my friend Dr. Thomas Neuville at Millersville, who recommended a former student with an intellectual disability, exactly the kind of perspective the council needed.

I put together a strong, diverse slate of candidates and submitted my recommendations. Then I waited.

Weeks went by. Then months. Nothing.

Finally, I called the executive director to ask what happened. He gave me the standard bureaucratic runaround. "It takes time," "the process is slow," "appointments can take six months."

Perhaps he had forgotten who he was talking to. I had been appointed in just a few weeks. I reminded him of his promise to take my recommendations seriously. He said he would "look into it."

A few weeks later, during a virtual council meeting, I saw the slate of candidates they were sending to the Governor's Office. Not a single person I recommended was on it.

It hit me hard. I realized in that moment what my role had really been: the token Black man on the recruitment committee. My presence had checked their box for diversity, but my work, my expertise, and my recommendations were ignored.

I decided then and there that I would resign and make it public.

I wrote a detailed resignation letter outlining my reasons and sent it to the executive director, the president, all council members, and a few public officials.

The response was immediate. Several SILC members reached out privately to express their support for my decision and to acknowledge that they, too, had been frustrated by the lack of diversity. Some even said they were considering resigning as well.

My resignation sparked a reckoning. SILC began to take diversity seriously and eventually made real changes.

And here's where the story takes a turn.

When one door closed, another one opened. The ending of a thing is the beginning of a thing.

My longtime colleague, Thomas Earle, CEO of Liberty Resources in Philadelphia, heard about my resignation.

He called me up and said, "Theo, National Council on Independent Living (NCIL) is going through the same thing SILC went through. I'm running for an at-large position on their board. You should run too. If we both get in, we can help make change from within."

He caught me at the perfect time. I had just walked away from SILC and was still fired up. We laughed about it and decided to do it.

We both ran for seats on the NCIL Board and were both elected.

What SILC meant for exclusion became the catalyst for my next chapter in leadership. I was no longer anyone's token. I was a trailblazer.

Chapter 4: The Great Senator Bob Casey

Senator Bob Casey, Jr., served as a United States Senator for 18 years. He lost his seat in 2024.

My final words to Senator Bob Casey at a recognition ceremony were these:

"I hope by now you have fully embraced the contributions you have made to improving the lives of millions of Americans.

People with disabilities and older Americans, both of whom I belong to. I owe you an enormous debt of gratitude.

I cannot imagine where we would be without your steadfast leadership and tireless advocacy on our behalf."

I meant every word!

On a personal level, Senator Casey played a significant role in shaping a crucial part of my life. It was the Senator who pulled me out of retirement, reminding me that my work was unfinished.

Because of that, I had the privilege of serving and working alongside some of the most extraordinary folks within the Biden Administration, working on historic advancements in home and community-based services, strengthening caregiving initiatives, finalizing the long-awaited Section 504 rules, and laying the groundwork for safer air travel for people with disabilities.

Those achievements are now under attack, but I draw strength from Senator Casey's example. His steadfastness reminds me that we do not give up when what we have built is threatened. We fight to protect it.

Senator Casey reminds me of another great leader I admired, the late President Jimmy Carter, a man whose life was his message. Both men inspire me to strive to be a better human being.

The connection with Senator actually goes back further than he knows.

In 1988, I attended the signing of Senate Bill 730, the Pennsylvania Americans with Disabilities Act, signed into law by his father, Governor Robert P. Casey, Sr.

That law changed the trajectory for people with disabilities in Pennsylvania.

Decades later, I would find myself working side by side with his son, continuing the legacy of that signature.

Let me share the backstory on how the Senator redirected my fourth life.

One night the phone rang. I was getting ready for bed when I heard the voice on the other end say, "Can you hold for Senator Casey?"

When he got on the line, he said, "Theo, I have had the pleasure of working with you for years. I know your heart and your commitment. That's why I've chosen you as one of this year's Trailblazers in honor of Black History Month."

I was speechless.

Every February, Senator Casey had recognized Black leaders across Pennsylvania for their impact in overcoming barriers and creating lasting change.

In 2022, as we emerged from the pandemic, he honored me by selecting me for this award.

I was not seeking this honor, but most of the significant things that happen to me happen when I am just busy helping others. This is an example of it.

A part of the event was watching the livestream (https://www.youtube.com/watch?v=JpOA8n1MqtI&t=7s) as Senator Casey announced my name and the reason, he selected me during his floor remarks commemorating Black History Month on February 14, 2022, for the Congressional Record.

He spoke my name and story, which is now officially entered into the Congressional Record.

He typically had another event in DC, but due to the pandemic, it became a virtual event, a ceremony entitled, Resilience in the Face of Adversity: A Black History Month Celebration (https://www.youtube.com/watch?v=-uYqEKMRGNM&t=3s) hosted by Sen. Bob Casey.

During the virtual event, the moderator asked me, "If you had the ear of decision makers in Washington, what would you tell them?"

Without much thought, I said, "More people with disabilities, who have lived experience, need to be elevated and appointed into positions of power in our government. Contrary to popular belief, we do exist."

A few weeks later, I was outside sun-gazing, as I often do, when I saw a voicemail on my phone from a "Mrs. White."

She said she was calling from the White House. I laughed and assumed it was spam.

A few days later, the message came to mind again. On a whim, I googled her name, and there she was, listed as a staff member in the White House Office of Presidential Appointments.

I called her back immediately.

"Theo," she said, "I was about to move on to the next person. Today was your last day to accept the nomination. Senator Casey recommended you for appointment to the National Council on Disability. Are you willing to accept?"

I was stunned and deeply moved.

Of course, I said yes.

A few weeks later, I received the official notice. President Biden had signed the appointment.

Here's the lesson in all this: I had spent years telling policymakers that people with disabilities must have a seat at the table, not just as advocates, but as decision makers.

Senator Casey not only listened, but he also acted.

And because he did, I had no choice but to come out of retirement and recommitted my life to service once again.

Chapter 5: The Perfect Fit

Getting into national issues was never part of my plan.

People often ask, "Theo, how do these things keep happening to you? What's your secret?"

Time after time, I give them the same answer, and time after time, they don't believe me.

I tell them two things.

First, like I shared earlier, most of the good things that have truly blessed my life were not things I went looking for. They just happened, usually while I was busy helping others.

Second, I tell them that I am always working to improve myself. I am always learning. And the more I learn, the more I realize how much I still don't know.

Anyway, back to my point about not seeking a national platform.

It was early in my career when I made an important decision. Actually, it happened during one of the National Independent Living Council (NCIL)'s Annual Independent Living (IL) Conferences.

Every year, NCIL coordinates an IL conference where thousands of leaders with and without disabilities gather in DC.

I was in my early thirties, deeply involved in my state work, when I attended that conference. I remember looking around the large lobby and seeing many national leaders, including Judy Heumann, Marca Bristo, Deidre Davis, Gina McDonald, Bob Michaels, and Don Calloway, to name a few.

I said to myself, "There are already plenty of great leaders doing national work. They don't need me."

So, I made a conscious decision that day to focus on my state of PA. That's why, when I later became Executive Director of NCIL, I wasn't widely known nationally, but everyone in Pennsylvania knew who I was.

Let's go back to when Thomas Earle and I were both appointed to NCIL's Board of Directors.

That experience is a perfect example of what I mean when I say I don't chase things. I get blessed while helping others.

We started our new roles on the NCIL Board by attending a two-day virtual board meeting and strategic planning retreat.

Day one began with a consultant reviewing NCIL's recent strategic planning results.

Now, remember when Thomas told me on that phone call that NCIL was having issues with inclusion? Let me share that backstory.

At a past NCIL's Annual IL Conference, a group of members from the BIPOC community, along with members of other marginalized communities, including LGBTQ+ advocates, interrupted the conference in protest. They said NCIL's leadership was not inclusive and that their voices were being left out.

Instead of acknowledging the truth, NCIL's leadership at that time, mostly white males with spinal cord injuries, pushed back and denied it.

Not long after, NCIL began losing members. People left because they had lost faith in leadership.

A quick update on that: since I became Executive Director, faith has been restored. Many former members are returning, and new members are joining every year.

So, after that leadership shake-up, NCIL began intentionally recruiting new leaders, people of color like Thomas and me, and others representing diverse identities: individuals who were blind, intellectually disabled, LGBTQ+, and more.

Finally, NCIL was serious about inclusion. This was our chance.

I began speaking up, sharing ideas, and action steps that they could make to create lasting change. I reminded everyone that diversity, equity, accessibility, and inclusion (DEAI) is not a one-time event. It's ongoing work. The kind that never ends.

To my surprise, there was no pushback. NCIL's leadership was ready to listen and to act.

That excited me. It's exactly what I was doing through my new consulting firm.

Then, as I sat listening to the consultant share more findings, she mentioned that NCIL was seeking a new Executive Director.

That caught my attention. It's rare to conduct strategic planning without an Executive Director in place. So, I asked why.

They explained that the interim Executive Director, Darrell Jones, was retiring.

Let me take a moment to recognize Darrell Jones. The IL movement owes her a lot. She is a pioneer and a trailblazer. From the start, she supported my hiring at NCIL and helped me transition into the role. **Thank you, Darrell.**

After that first day ended, I was lying in bed, thinking about everything that had happened. Then it hit me: I could do more for NCIL as its Executive Director than as a board member.

I was already mentally and spiritually coming out of retirement. I had just recommitted myself by accepting President Biden's appointment to the National Council on Disability (NCD).

So, I called Thomas Earle and shared my idea. He said, "Theo, that's a great idea. You have my full support." To this day, I still wonder if he already had that in mind before the first call from him. He never told me, and I never asked.

The next day, I resigned from the NCIL board and explained why.

Everyone was supportive, and the President, Kent Crenshaw, accepted my resignation with encouragement. He told me I could always come back to the board someday.

The rest, as they say, is history.

I was unanimously hired as NCIL's Executive Director, and I started on February 2, 2023.

I now had what could be seen as two full-time positions: one at NCIL and one with NCD. Both allowed me to shape national policy and improve the lives of people with disabilities every single day. How amazing is that?

Since I now have more years behind me than ahead, I have become selective about what I take on. Everything I do has to matter. It has to make a difference.

And these two roles with NCIL and NCD, they do. It is a perfect fit.

When I took over at NCIL, I had years of experience fixing struggling organizations. In Pennsylvania alone, I had taken over at least three Centers for Independent Living that were on the brink of collapse.

The Rehabilitation Service Administration (RSA), now the Administration on Community Living (ACL), staff often called me when a center was in trouble. ACL is where centers receive federal funding.

Most of the time, I had to make tough decisions, sometimes letting go of staff to remove old baggage and rebuild from scratch.

So naturally, I wondered if I would need to take the same approach at NCIL.

However, when I came aboard, Darrell Jones, NCIL's Interim Executive Director, had already built a strong core team.

Now it was my turn to see if they would follow my lead.

I have always believed what leadership expert John Maxwell teaches; positional authority will only take you so far. True leadership is earned, not given.

I needed to know if this core group would grow to respect my leadership, not just follow orders, but willingly go into battle with me.

As I write this, we're still figuring some things out together. But one thing I'm sure of is their deep commitment and passion for NCIL's mission and vision.

Commitment and passion: two things I have always looked for when hiring anyone. Because everything else can be taught or caught.

The Board, on the other hand, was a little more complicated.

For example, one of my executive committee members had applied for the very position I was now holding. When I was hired, he wasn't.

It turned out he held on to that resentment. He even called a secret "special meeting" to criticize my performance, comparing what he would have done to what I was doing.

Another board member questioned why I wasn't present at this meeting, and that's how I found out about it.

I filed a grievance, and the member eventually resigned from the Executive Committee.

Then there was another board member, someone I initially thought was an ally. He was also an Executive Director of a federally funded center, one that had its grant terminated by ACL who alleged him of financial mismanagement.

He carried a grudge against ACL, and he wanted me to share in that anger.

But I refused. I had no reason to hate people that I had no bad experiences with them. That decision changed everything between us.

He became openly hostile, blaming me and NCIL for not fighting ACL on his behalf. Even after we created a task force to review ACL's actions and found that ACL could have handled some steps differently. He refused to acknowledge it.

Eventually, his behavior crossed the line into harassment. I had to tell the President that if he didn't intervene, I would take legal action. Thankfully, it stopped.

I am still working to find my sweet spot with the NCIL Board. That place where we are all moving together in the same direction, with the same purpose.

The NCIL board is made up of strong, accomplished leaders, CEOs, Executive Directors, and disability leaders, each with their own way of doing things. Sometimes they want me to do things their way, forgetting that I have led before, that I too have my own way.

One of my greatest leadership strengths has always been trusting my instincts, that inner voice that guides me toward the right direction and vision. When I feel supported, I can operate fully in that space, and amazing things happen. That's my sweet spot.

Thankfully, today, with a new President and a stronger, more diverse board culture, I can see real movement in a better direction. We are starting to find our rhythm, to believe in each other.

Whether I will still be in this seat when this book is published, only time will tell. But one thing I do know, the foundation is stronger, and the mission continues forward.

The Call.

"Hello, this is Judy Heumann calling. I was just calling to say congratulations on your new position and hope to be able to be in touch with you and see what help I and some other people could be."

As I mentioned, I officially began my new role as Executive Director of NCIL on February 2, 2023.

Just a few weeks later, on February 15, I received the above quoted call that would leave a lasting mark on my heart.

It was from Judy Heumann.

I missed the call, but she left me a voice message.

Now, here's the backstory, and not many people know this. I had never met Judy face-to-face.

I had seen her many times at NCIL conferences over the years. The first time I saw her, I just watched her from afar. I was in awe. I wanted to go up and introduce myself, but I didn't. Believe it or not, I was nervous.

That's something I often tell young leaders now: never let fear keep you from speaking to someone you admire.

People love being approached by those who respect them. They enjoy mentoring. Judy probably would have welcomed a great conversation with me, but back then, it wasn't about her. It was about my own fear.

And that fear robbed me of what might have been a beautiful connection with one of the most iconic leaders of our movement.

So, when that call came, it meant the world to me.

When I called Judy back, we spoke at length. She wanted to reconnect with NCIL, an organization she helped build.

Many people forget that Judy was one of the original signers of NCIL's Articles of Incorporation. She believed deeply in NCIL's mission and served faithfully for years, especially through her work on the International Committee.

Our conversation was rich and easy, like we had known each other forever. We talked about the future, about building a bridge between the pioneers of the Independent Living Movement and the next younger generation.

We both admitted something that day: we had more years behind us than in front of us.

We agreed that it was time to be intentional about mentoring new leaders. That was the mission we shared: to pass the torch while it could still light the way for others.

We planned to talk again soon to strategize and dream.

But that call, that one conversation, would be our first and last.

Just a few weeks later, on March 4, 2023, Judy passed away.

Her death shook me deeply. It was a devastating loss, not just for the disability community but for people around the world. Judy Heumann was more than a leader; she was a movement all by herself. The mother of the independent movement.

At NCIL that year, we honored her legacy by creating The Judy Heumann Award.

We also kept her presence close. Two of Judy's motorized wheelchairs were donated to NCIL, and during the award presentation, we placed one of them on stage beside me.

It felt like Judy was still there watching, guiding, reminding us to lead on.

Judy always seemed unstoppable, eternal even. It's hard to imagine the movement without her. But her spirit lives on in our advocacy, our work, and our unwavering belief that disability rights are, in fact, human rights.

Around the same time, I began at NCIL, I was also sworn in to my presidential appointment to the National Council on Disability (NCD).

I took my oath before Chair Andres Gallegos, a brilliant and compassionate leader who carried himself with grace and power.

For those who may not know, NCD is an independent federal agency that advises the President and Congress on disability policy. It's the same agency that drafted the original framework of the Americans with Disabilities Act (ADA).

So, sitting there, being sworn in, I couldn't help but think: I was walking the same path as the giants whose shoulders we all stand on.

People like Justin Dart Jr., the man in the cowboy hat whose quiet power changed the world. Justin didn't just help pass the ADA; he embodied it. His mantra, "Lead on," became a battle cry for all of us. If you recall, in my third life, Justin was one of my mentors.

Then there was Lex Frieden, who helped write the ADA and served as Chair of the NCD. Lex had that rare combination of intellect and humility. You listened when he spoke because you could tell he cared deeply about getting it right.

And Marca Bristo, fierce, fearless, and brilliant. The first person with a visible disability to chair NCD, Marca believed in leading with purpose and heart. She taught us all that disability rights are human rights.

These were not just leaders. They were legends.

As time went on, a new generation of leaders joined NCD and carried that same torch in new ways.

Ari Ne'eman, an autistic self-advocate, brought youthful fire and deep wisdom beyond his years. Alice Wong, with her ventilator and her boundless creativity, reminded the world that visibility is power. Fernando Torres-Gil, a fellow polio survivor, brought the insight of a scholar and the compassion of a man who had lived the struggle himself.

Then there's Claudia Gordon, a deaf attorney from Jamaica who broke barriers that never should have been there in the first place. She later became NCD Chair, continuing the tradition of lived experience leading the way.

I also think about early members like Joni Eareckson Tada, Nanette Fabray, and Henry Viscardi Jr., all of whom used their platforms to challenge perceptions and expand opportunity.

And people like Chester Finn, Lynnae Ruttledge, Neil Romano, and Clyde Terry, advocates who reminded us that leadership doesn't come from perfection, but from persistence.

And then there was Andrés Gallegos, another quadriplegic, who became Chair of NCD and one of my dearest friends. From the very beginning, Andrés took me under his wing.

Our friendship grew fast and deep. Our wives even became friends, both knowing what it meant to love and care for men with our kind of injuries.

When Andrés passed away, it hit me hard. His loss left a hole in NCD and in me. I'm not sure it will ever be filled.

But his legacy remains, one of justice, integrity, and courage.

Today, NCD continues to evolve. Each transition brings in new leaders, people shaped by their own lived experiences and their unshakable commitment to disability justice.

Shawn Kennemer, now Acting Chair, is a seasoned advocate and CEO of Bakersfield ARC in California. He brings decades of experience serving people with disabilities and a deep understanding of what real inclusion looks like.

Emily Voorde, who served as Vice Chair, brought a new energy grounded in education policy and youth empowerment. She worked in the White House Office of Public Engagement, carrying with her the belief that the government should listen to its people.

Among the current members, each brings something vital.

Hoskie Benally Jr., a member of the Navajo Nation and legally blind, has spent his life advancing disability rights in Indigenous communities. Sascha Bittner, who lives with cerebral palsy, is a fierce voice for home care and workers' rights.

Risa "Jaz" Rifkind represents a new kind of leadership. She is creative, civic-minded, and focused on shifting power into the hands of people with disabilities.

And then there's Neil Romano, whose long service and insight remind us that progress is built on both vision and consistency. Neil is a perfect example of why it shouldn't matter whether you are a Republican or a Democrat, but rather how you genuinely serve the good of all people. He is a man I highly respect and enjoy working with.

And somewhere in that mix, there's me.

A man who started out as a poor kid from Georgia, once told he wasn't college material, now sitting on a federal council shaping national disability policy.

That's the beauty of NCD, it's a table where lived experience sits in the seat of power.

It's where pain, perseverance, and purpose meet policy.

And that's what real progress looks like.

Both Claudia and Emily resigned after the new administration took office.

As a Biden appointee, I was sure that I would be replaced. So far, I am still here.

I wasn't going to resign. I came to make a difference and still believed in doing just that: making a difference.

Chapter 6: Meeting the Moment - Anna

When I first met Anna Perng, I had just stepped into my role as NCIL's new Executive Director. I was still getting my bearings when an invitation arrived from the White House.

Anna, who served as a Senior Advisor in the White House Office of Public Engagement and acted as President Biden's primary liaison to the aging and disability communities, had invited me for a private tour of the White House.

From that very first meeting, I could tell Anna was the real deal, kind, authentic, and full of purpose. I have always been drawn to people like that, and we hit it off immediately.

Anna recognized the importance of ensuring that NCIL's voice was heard on key policies and initiatives the Biden Administration was putting forth that affected people with disabilities.

She made sure NCIL had access to the People's House, the White House to ensure a true sense of inclusion and belonging. For the first time in a long time, it felt like the door wasn't just open to us, but that we had a rightful seat at the table.

That first invitation became the beginning of a professional friendship that I came to value deeply. Whenever there was a need for feedback, insight, or lived experience, Anna thought of me. She knew I would speak truth, even when it was uncomfortable.

Here are just a few of those "meeting the moment" White House events and other key interactions that shaped me during my fourth life.

Fourth of July Celebration – July 4, 2023

My first official White House event under Anna's invitation was the Fourth of July celebration on the South Lawn. The air was alive with music and fireworks, but what struck me most was being surrounded by so many people who had worked for years to make this nation more inclusive and accessible.

July is always an exciting month for people with disabilities. It is our Independence Day! It is the month of the ADA's signing.

Lowering Health Care Costs Event – July 7, 2023

Just days later, I was back at the White House for an event focused on lowering health care costs. It was one of the first moments I realized how intentional this Administration was about including disability perspectives in every major policy conversation.

People with disabilities MUST be at the table.

Accessible Transportation Convening with Vice President Harris – July 11, 2023

That same month, I joined Vice President Kamala Harris and Secretary Pete Buttigieg for a White House convening on accessible transportation.

I had the honor of offering remarks on the urgent need to fix the air travel experience for people with disabilities.

I shared how I stopped flying due to the harm it caused me, which resulted in my not being able to go on a dream vacation to Paris with my wife, and how not flying has negatively impacted my career choices.

Anna made sure everything went smoothly that day, even creating a private space inside the White House for me to record a live Joyce Bender podcast episode I had previously committed to.

I remember telling Joyce on the live broadcast, "I am speaking to you from the White House." We both laughed.

Afterward, Anna sent me a note that I'll never forget:

> "Thank you so much for sharing so honestly and personally about how inaccessible air travel has impacted you. We really appreciate your willingness to get to the heart of this issue in a way that will help the broader public understand the significance of what the Biden-Harris Administration is trying to accomplish, fulfilling the promise of the ADA."

That same day, my son met the Vice President. It was one of those moments that stick with you. We captured the moment in a picture.

ADA 33rd Anniversary Roundtable – July 26, 2023

Later that month, Anna invited me back for the 33rd Anniversary of the Americans with Disabilities Act, a roundtable at the White House. It was both a celebration and a working session, focusing on new rulemaking and unfinished business related to equality.

This was real action that had a significant impact.

Home and Community-Based Care Discussion – December 12, 2023

In December, I joined senior officials for an off-the-record conversation on home and community-based care. The same morning, the White House streamed a virtual event highlighting progress from the American Rescue Plan's HCBS investments across all 50 states. (Event url: https://www.youtube.com/watch?v=a3_8_JA9sFI).

During this event, I was surprised by Governor Shapiro of Pennsylvania, who thanked me on the livestream for my work on behalf of PA citizens.

Anna followed up after the event, writing to me:

"Thank you for calling out the fact that disabled people must be at the table, and that HCBS is about dignity, and it is also about economic self-sufficiency, independence, and the ability to contribute and realize one's potential, all the things, as you said, non-disabled people take for granted."

Black History Month Reception – February 6, 2024

The following February, I attended a Black History Month reception at the White House. Anna sent me another kind message that day:

"Theo, the best part of this job is being able to work with leaders like you and bringing our community to the People's House so we can affect change together. You have impacted so many policies, and I hope you will feel proud on Thursday!!!"

Air Travelers with Disabilities Announcement – February 29, 2024

That month ended with a powerful event: a White House and U.S. Department of Transportation announcement about new protections for air travelers with disabilities, with remarks from Secretary Buttigieg and Senator Tammy Duckworth.

(Event url: https://www.youtube.com/watch?v=D9Y-WJLZ3Ts).

I had stated at an earlier event that I didn't think in my lifetime, I would see the kind of changes in air travel for people with disabilities that would be needed for me to travel by air again.

I had to change that statement because of the final rules. Maybe I would live to see it.

I was so happy to pull this statement back, but now the Trump Administration is trying to rescind all of this progress – we can't go back!

Care Economy All-Call – April 23, 2024

In April, I participated in the White House All-Call on the Care Economy, advancing long-term care initiatives that prioritize independence, family caregivers, and community living. See video by visiting here: https://www.youtube.com/watch?v=cTJ77Z39nOw.

Meeting with Olena Zelenska, First Lady of Ukraine – July 10, 2024

On July 10, 2024, I had the honor of joining Alison Barkoff, the ACL Administrator and Assistant Secretary for Aging, as well as several high-level officials from the Department of State at this high-level event. View video by visiting here: https://www.instagram.com/reel/C9SDZTsJIFT.

Olena Zelenska, wife of President Volodymyr Zelenskyy of Ukraine, came to the US seeking guidance on how we establish the IL movement in the US.

Due to the war with Russia, many veterans returned with life-long injuries, head injuries, loss of limbs, and there were also non-veterans, those injured through the bombings, children and adults now facing a lifetime of living with disabilities.

Our group from the US provided the Ukrainian delegation with some advice and direction, as Ukraine is transitioning towards a community living model rather than an institutional one. Ukraine is seeking ways to improve the treatment of people with disabilities.

As I sat there, I was quickly reminded that although we still have much to do here in the U.S. to advance the rights of people with disabilities, persons with disabilities are far better situated than in other countries like Ukraine.

Ukraine has much to do as Veterans return with disabilities, and children are devastated with lifelong disabling conditions.

I shared this with the First Lady:

"How you see people with disabilities will determine how you treat us. If you see us as less than, less valuable, pity us, and see us as charity cases that we only take from society and do not contribute to society, then you will not treat us like you treat yourselves".

During another event, I was invited to virtually speak at an event of the Russian delegation of community disability leaders from Russia.

In both of these events, I learned something. It didn't matter if they were from Ukraine or Russia; these were individuals trying to figure things out in the aftermath of a terrifying ordeal.

I had mixed feelings. I was glad I didn't live in these war-torn countries, but at the same time, I know America doesn't love people like me as much as we love America.

It is something I continually struggle with.

25th Olmstead Anniversary – June 20, 2024

This was an extraordinary event! It represented an Act that has provided freedom of countless people with disabilities being freed for institutionalization. U.S. Department of Health and Human Services (HHS) and U.S. Department of Justice event commemorating the 25th anniversary of the Olmstead decision.

Disability Pride Month Convening – July 29, 2024

That summer, I joined the White House Disability Pride Month Convening, a powerful gathering of disabled leaders and advocates. It was about pride, progress, and the promise that this country should work for everyone.

89th Anniversary of the Social Security Act – August 14, 2024

I was honored to present at the 89th Anniversary of the Social Security Act, alongside Commissioner Martin O'Malley and Representative John Larson, discussing the future of this vital program.

Do your research on this one. You will be surprised by how much the Biden Administration worked on positive changes with SSA and SSI.

ADA 34th Anniversary & Disability Pride Reception – September 9, 2024

Another special moment came that Fall when I attended the White House Disability Pride & 34th Anniversary of the ADA reception. These milestones always remind me how advocacy, persistence, and unity can truly move mountains.

Special Olympics Dinner – December 10, 2024

I received an invitation to the Special Olympics Dinner at the White House. It was a night filled with joy, respect, and celebration of what inclusion really looks like in practice. President Biden provided remark. Maria Shriver was also in attendance, and we were entertained by CeCe Winans.

Reflections on Anna

Through all of this, one thing stayed constant: Anna's heart and dedication to ensure that people with disabilities' voices were heard.

She didn't just open doors; she ensured that NCIL and the disabled community walked and rolled through them.

She believed in partnership, not tokenism. She understood that policy was personal.

And she knew how to bring the disability community's lived experience straight into the center of power, with grace, strategy, and authenticity.

If you ask me what leadership in government should look like, I would say: It looks a lot like Anna Perng. **Thank you, Anna.**

Chapter 7: We Can't Go Back - Alison

When I first met Alison Barkoff, she was serving as the Acting Administrator for the Administration for Community Living (ACL) and Assistant Secretary for Aging.

I met her not long after becoming NCIL's new Executive Director, right around the same time I met Anna.

From the very beginning, Alison struck me as genuine, the kind of person who doesn't need to prove she cares. You can just tell.

But before I even met her, I was being warned by a NCIL board member. He told me ACL had a history of favoring the aging network over the independent living network.

You know the story: Area Agencies on Aging (AAAs) versus Centers for Independent Living (CILs).

I listened. But it didn't sit right with me.

Because here's how I have always looked at it. We are all aging into disability. The divide between aging and disability makes no sense.

When I finally met Alison, I realized she saw it the same way. We hit it off immediately.

From that point forward, we were partners in bridging that gap, tearing down that invisible wall between the two worlds that should have always been one.

Alison is one of those rare people who brings intellect, heart, and lived experience into the same room.

When she speaks, it isn't just academic talk. It's truth, rooted in both policy and real life. You can feel it. I often told her this.

One of the things I had an opportunity to work with Alison on, I refer to as a game-changer.

Alison was taking on history. For the first time in fifty years, our country was rewriting the Section 504 rule of the Rehabilitation Act.

That law, passed in 1973, is the backbone of civil rights for people with disabilities. It's what says we have the same right as anyone else to live, learn, work, and receive services without discrimination.

But Alison understood this wasn't just about updating old language. She knew it was a chance to fix what had been broken for decades, how doctors see us, how systems fail us, how technology leaves us behind.

She worked hand-in-hand with the Office for Civil Rights, making sure this rule wouldn't just look good on paper, but that it would work in real life.

For months, she held listening sessions, took public comments, and opened the door wide for the disability community.

Thousands of advocates and everyday people shared their stories. And when the final rule came out in 2024, Alison called it "disability rights history." She was right.

This was the first major update since the 1970s, and it brought Section 504 into the modern world.

On May 1, 2024, Alison and I stood side by side at the event marking the release of final rules. On stage with HHS Secretary Bacerra, HHS Announced the Finalization of a Rule Prohibiting Discrimination of the Basis of Disability (https://www.youtube.com/watch?v=mYliKkvNi98).

I remember that moment clearly; the air in the room was charged with excitement, hope, exhaustion, and relief. We had been fighting this battle for years.

When it was my turn to speak, I didn't read from a script. I just spoke from my heart:

"We are punching ableism in the face, and hopefully it's going to be a knockout punch, and it won't get up again. But if it gets up again, it will be because we didn't do what we were supposed to do. It will take people like us to fight it."

That line came straight from the heart because that's how it felt.

I have seen ableism dressed up in too many forms: in hospitals, classrooms, policies, and politics. It keeps getting back up. But that day, I believed we gave it a knockout punch.

In 2025, Alison and I shared another platform, a national briefing called "What You Can Do to Stop the Attack on Section 504."

Some states were already filing lawsuits trying to weaken parts of the 504 new rules. We both knew how dangerous that was.

If they succeeded, decades of progress would be lost.

At that event, Alison brought the government's voice, and I brought the community's voice. Together, we told the world what was at stake and how to stand up for the promise of Section 504.

For me, this work is never just professional. It's personal.

I became disabled as a teenager after a football injury. I have lived what it means to be institutionalized in a nursing home.

To have people decide your worth for you. That's why I fight. That's why I lead.

That's why Section 504 matters so deeply.

It's not just a rule. It's a promise. It says: we belong everywhere. We can't go back! **Thank you, Alison!**

Chapter 8: Vice President Harris

I met Vice President Kamala Harris for the first time at the Accessible Transportation Convening Roundtable on July 11, 2023, at the White House.

There she was, seated right next to who could one day be President himself, Secretary of Transportation Pete Buttigieg.

The room was filled with key players, advocates, and policymakers. Everyone gathered to provide feedback on the Administration's upcoming air travel safety rules for people with disabilities.

Our name plates were perfectly laid out across the long White House conference table. Sitting beside me was Tony Coelho, the legendary "Architect of the ADA." Next to him, Vice President Harris herself.

Each of us was asked to give a brief five-minute statement. I sat there, listening to the elegant, well-rehearsed remarks from others, waiting for my turn. I was almost last, so I had plenty of time to think, to listen, and to realize that no prepared speech could say what I needed to say. I've never been one for scripts anyway.

Finally, my turn came.

I looked around the room, took a breath, and began,

"Thank you, President Harris, for inviting me here today…"

The room went silent for a half-second before laughter erupted. Yes, I accidentally called her President Harris.

I quickly corrected myself and smiled, saying,

"Well, maybe I'm just being prophetic."

For a brief moment, I was the comic relief. And honestly? I didn't mind it. A few months later, when she announced her run for President, I thought, maybe I really was prophetic after all. That would have been a great story for this book.

Once the laughter settled, I got serious. I told my story.

I shared how I had to stop flying early in my career because airlines repeatedly damaged my power wheelchair, dropping it, mishandling it, and leaving me stranded. I spoke about how that loss of mobility impacted my professional life, keeping me from conferences and opportunities across the country.

Then I told them about the hardest part, how I couldn't take my wife to Paris for her dream trip. I had to stay home while she went with a friend because I couldn't risk flying. She understood. She knew how dangerous it could be to be stranded in another country without a working wheelchair.

I said, "That's what ableism looks like in real life. I am not here today just for me. I am here for the next generation of people with disabilities who deserve better."

My words landed. Vice President Harris looked me in the eye, visibly moved, and she thanked me for sharing my story and apologized for what I had experienced. Her sincerity was real; you could feel it.

Almost a year later, on February 29, 2024, I was invited back to Washington for a press conference where Secretary Buttigieg, alongside Senator Tammy Duckworth, officially announced the Final Air Travel Safety Rules (https://www.youtube.com/watch?v=D9Y-WJLZ3Ts).

During his remarks, Secretary Buttigieg quoted my story. When it was my turn to speak, I said something I never thought I would say again:

"Maybe I was wrong. Maybe I will be able to travel again in my lifetime."

Those words became part of the Administration's social media campaign promoting the new rules. It felt like a full-circle moment. My hope restored.

Unfortunately, as I write this, the new administration and several major airlines are trying to roll back those same hard-fought rules.

My message to them, and to all of us, is simple:

"We can't let that happen. We've come too far to go back."

Chapter 9: President Biden

I met President Joe Biden on several occasions. Still, none were as impactful as the day I received a personal invitation to meet with him one-on-one and have my photograph taken with him. It is the picture on the back cover of this book.

A few great leaders were there that day, waiting in line for their moment to speak with the President. I found myself sitting right behind another great man, Tony Coelho, known as the Architect of the ADA.

I remember thinking to myself, I should be in line waiting to meet Tony as well. Tony is a hero to me. If you don't know Tony Coelho, google him. You'll be glad you did.

When Tony stepped up, he and President Biden embraced like old friends who had been through battles together. I wanted to take a picture of that moment, but we weren't allowed. Only the official White House photographer could capture those memories.

Then it was my turn.

As I approached the President, we shook hands. Of course, I fumbled over my words, something about the weight of the moment and the man standing before me, but I regrouped and shared what was truly on my heart: how deeply grateful I was for his commitment to supporting people with disabilities throughout his administration.

President Biden leaned in close, looked me straight in the eye, and whispered:

"You have lived an extraordinary life of bravery. You are a courageous man."

Those words froze me in time. You know those moments in movies when everything slows down, and a lifetime of memories flashes by in an instant? That's what happened. And then the world moved again.

My journey, every struggle, every victory flashed before me.

FROM SHACK TO WHITE HOUSE: A MEMOIR OF FOUR LIVES

Here I was, a young kid who once grew up in poverty, in a little shack, just wanting to be noticed and not forgotten.

Now, standing in the White House, and the most powerful man in the free world was telling me I was brave and courageous.

In that moment, I felt my journey come full circle.

We posed for a photo together, just the President and me. Captured by the White House photographer. That photo now hangs above my office desk.

Every time I look up at it, I can still hear his words in my mind, as clear as that day:

"You are a courageous man."

And every time I do, I smile and whisper back! **Thank you, Joe. I am still fighting!**

Part V: Bonus Hits - Lessons Along the Way

By the time you have lived four lives, you don't walk away without a few lessons imprinted into your way of life.

Some lessons I learned the easy way. Mostly, I learned the hard way, through mistakes, setbacks, heartbreak, and pain.

I first heard this from my pastor, Dr. Ashe, "A setback is just a setup for a comeback". It has stayed with me, and I pass it on here.

But here's the truth: every one of those lessons shaped me. They guided me as I became a man, a father, a leader, and an advocate.

They became the "Theo-isms" that people around me began to repeat, small bits of wisdom drawn from lived experiences.

This section is different from the rest of my story.

These aren't just memories; they are the truths I carried out of them. They are the things I wish someone had told me when I was fifteen, or twenty-five, or even fifty.

Some are simple. Some are hard. All of them are real.

Before I close, I want to share with you the lessons I have learned along the way.

Not because I have lived a perfect life, far from it, but because life has been generous enough to teach me, and I believe wisdom only matters if it's passed on.

Theo-ism: *A sacrifice isn't a sacrifice unless it costs you something, and I'm not talking about money.*

Redefining Success

I used to think success meant big titles, money, or recognition. Life taught me otherwise.

Success, I have learned, is the steady realization of pre-determined goals you have intentionally set for yourself. Not dreams, dreams are fantasies. Vision without goals is fantasy; you only dream about things.

These are "one day folks." We all know folks like this. They start in their twenties, talking about what they will do one day. One day, I will do this or that, and they are still saying the same thing in their forties.

Goals without vision are drudgery. It's the routines you get used to. It's when your job just becomes a 9-to-5 grind. You do it, but it's just drudgery, a weight you carry.

The secret is marrying the two, writing them down, making them measurable, and moving with intention.

Here is a bonus thought: I believe that there are two kinds of dreamers. One is the Reality Dreamer, and the other is the Fantasy Dreamer. The Reality Dreamer dreams and then puts themselves in a position of making that dream a reality.

The Fantasy Dreamer dreams but continues to be "one day folks," I mentioned.

They continually talk about what one day they are going to do but never put themselves in a position to make it happen. It becomes just a fantasy to them.

Theo-ism: *Vision without goals is fantasy, goals without vision quickly become drudgery, but when you have vision and goals, you have a mission, and then you can really make things happen.*

The Power of "You Said"

This is something I learned as a minister. The Power of the you said.

It's when someone comes to you with a problem. It could be anything. Let's say it's a marriage problem, and they say, I think my wife is going to divorce me.

And as a counselor, you tell them the things they need to do to get their wife back.

Suddenly, it becomes too much work. "I don't want to do all that, they say."

Then, I, as the minister, I can use the power of the you said. "You said you wanted your wife back". That is why you came here; so, step up and do the necessary work.

I have learned to use "the power of the you said."

No one succeeds alone. Every step I have taken, someone has held me accountable to the words I spoke.

The power of "You said" has pushed me past my excuses, past the temptation to quit, and toward the finish line.

Theo-ism: *Don't let the words you speak roll so easily off your lips; words you say should have power and become action.*

Two Ears, One Mouth

As a kid, I learned the hard way that talking too much can get you in trouble.

As a leader, I learned that listening gets you further than speaking.

People can easily mistake silence for wisdom, but as soon as you open your mouth, you reveal the truth: your lack of wisdom.

I have seen these many times over my career. In board meetings, committee meetings, city council meetings, and even in the highest place in government, at White House meetings.

Just because you are the loudest in the room doesn't make you the wisest in the room.

Theo-ism: *This is not Theo-ism, but I use it a lot. God gave us two ears and one mouth for a reason; use them in that order.*

Pick Your Battles

Not every fight is yours to fight. Sometimes, your best defense is your reputation, the life you have already lived.

Sometimes, let the people who truly know you speak up for you.

Many times, in my life, someone has accused me of something or fed untruths about me. I have learned not to try to dispel it immediately.

Others, who know me, speak up and say, "That doesn't sound like something Theo would say or do."

Theo-ism: *Live so that when someone lies about you, others will come to your defense.*

Words That Matter

I have come to value certain words: accountability, reliability, dependability, integrity, and responsibility. Words mean little unless the life you live proves them true.

Just don't use these words without understanding what they mean operationally. Learn what they mean and put them into action every single day. You won't be perfect, strive to be better.

Integrity is one of my favorite words. Do your best to maintain it. We will say we will do something so easily, sometime hoping that the person we say it to will forget.

We are not perfect, sometimes life happens, and we can't deliver on our word, but keep your integrity intact by going to that person and ask them to forgive you and let them know genuinely what happened.

Theo-ism: *Integrity is when your words are consistent with what you do.*

Challenges and Failure

Challenges don't break you. They build you. They make you. Failure isn't an end. It's a doorway to new beginnings. My worst setbacks have been setups for comebacks.

When you fail, and you will. Take a pause and evaluate the failure. What can you learn from it?

If you don't, surely there is a good chance you will repeat it.

Theo-ism: *Don't fear failure. Fear not learning from it.*

Making God Smile

I make plans. God smiles. He adjusts them. I have learned not to resent that, but to smile with Him.

When life rewrites my schedule, I have learned to flow with it.

We all want to believe that we are in complete control of the direction our lives will go. At the age of 15, I had many plans for my life. Little did I know.

Theo-ism: *I have asked this question many times. Why me? The answer is always another question. Why not you?*

Recognition vs. Impact

Too many people get stuck asking, "Who gets the credit?" I have seen real change happen only when the work matters more than the spotlight.

When you don't care who gets the credit, you can do some amazing things.

I have accomplished many things, some of which I have shared in this book, while others I have never even mentioned to colleagues throughout my career, that these things were achieved by me.

Just do the work!

Theo-ism: *If lives are being changed, does it really matter who gets the credit?*

Living Well

"Independent living is not the same as living well independently." I coined this phrase many years ago.

It is still true today and will be tomorrow.

Living well independently is about joy, connection, and meaning, not just a place to stay, but also one that is not confined to an institution or nursing home.

Too often, we stop at getting people out of institutions, and we feel we have finished the work.

No, there is still unfinished work to be done.

Living well means different things to different folks at different times in their lives.

What it means to me is different than what it means to you.

Living well independently to me right now is finally finishing a lifelong dream of writing this book. It meant something entirely different a few years ago.

Theo-ism: *Don't measure life by where you live, but by how well you live.*

Be a Guide.

Knowledge is meant to be shared. I have lived long enough to know that mentoring or guiding someone else is the surest way to give your pain, your victories, and your story a purpose.

So often it will allow you just not to **go through**, but to **grow through** some extraordinary life moments, good or bad.

Theo-ism: *What you have learned should be eagerly shared with others.*

Remember the Mission

Money tempts. Recognition distracts. But if you lose sight of your mission, you lose yourself.

Theo-ism: *Your mission is your compass. It should guide you like a north star.*

For Alice!

During the final stretch of writing this book, the disability community lost **Alice Wong**, one of its brightest lights.

Her passing hit us all hard. Alice didn't just advocate, she shifted the mindset of all of us, especially folks who never or rarely interacted with the disabled community.

She spoke truth with courage, creativity, and a fire that made even the biggest systems pay attention.

I didn't know her personally the way some did, but her work shaped the world I had to navigate in my Third and Fourth Life.

She opened doors, pushed conversations, and refused to let our community be invisible. Alice made space for voices like mine and voices far too often ignored.

When I learned she was gone, I felt that familiar ache we all get when a giant leaves us.

It reminded me why we fight so hard.

Why we keep telling our stories.

Why we keep pushing the world to see us fully.

So, as I close this memoir, I want to say her name with gratitude.

Thank you, Alice.

You showed so many of us what it means to live boldly, fiercely, and unapologetically disabled.

Epilogue

When I look back over my life, from that little shack where it all began to the halls of the White House, one thing stands clear: I did not get here alone.

I have been called many things in my life: visionary, leader, advocate, and fighter. But before all that, I was simply Theo, a son, a brother, a husband, a father, and a man, even a coach.

When I say my family saved my life, I mean it in the most literal sense. They pulled me out of a nursing home when I was fifteen years old. They saw a future for me when the world saw none.

My sisters, Annie and Gladys, gathered what little money the family had and brought me to Pennsylvania.

That one act changed everything. It was the first miracle of many that would come through the people I love.

My brothers, who carried me down three flights of stairs just so I could feel the sun on my face. They taught me what love looks like in action.

To my first cousin, Pearlie Ragsdale, who truly saw me before my accident as unforgettable. And all my other extended family who stood by me when times were hard, you are all part of my story.

To my wife, Roe, my partner in every sense, thank you for loving me through every version of myself, and there are many. The version that causes me to be alone in the quietness of my own mind. Something that is not about you at all. It comes from so many years of being alone in a body that doesn't physically function, but a mind that does.

I didn't have any other choice but to learn to live that way. I know it has caused you pain, so forgive me for that.

But we have been through storms and sunshine, and through it all, you stood by me. You helped me find my way when I was lost, and you reminded me that courage isn't always loud; sometimes it's just quiet faith that tomorrow will be better.

And then there are my two greatest joys: my children. My daughter, Kimmi, who cried the day I proposed to her mother for the second time. That moment is forever etched in my heart. In her tears, I saw her love, her hope, and the bond between us as father and daughter. I never felt closer to her than in that moment, my little girl.

And my son, Theo II, many say he is the spitting image of me, and I can see it too. He is strong, confident, and, among all his issues, he is kind.

I could never toss a baseball back and forth with him like other dads, but he never seemed to care. To him, I was still the greatest athletic dad in the world. Through his eyes, I learned that fatherhood isn't defined by what you can do, but by how you show up with love, patience, and pride. I did my best to show up!

To my family, blood and chosen, you know who you are. I won't name anyone, because I would surely leave someone out. You have lifted me higher than I could ever climb alone. You have believed in me when I doubted myself. You have been my safe place in a world that isn't always kind to people like me.

Every title I have held: Executive Director, Board Member, Advisor, or Presidential Appointee has meant little compared to the title of family. Because when the lights go down and the crowd fades, it's family that remains.

To my family, those here and those who have passed on, thank you for walking with me. Every door I opened, every speech I gave, every policy I fought for. Your fingerprints are all over it.

Memoir Glossary

ACL (Administration for Community Living): A federal agency under the U.S. Department of Health and Human Services that focuses on older adults and people with disabilities. I worked closely with ACL during my time leading NCIL and NCD, primarily when Alison Barkoff served as Acting Administrator. ACL's mission to connect aging and disability communities lined up perfectly with my own belief that we are all aging into disability.

ADA (Americans with Disabilities Act): Passed in 1990, this law changed everything. It made discrimination against people with disabilities illegal. The ADA gave me, and millions of others, the right to access buildings, transportation, jobs, and services, and to live independently. Every time I roll through an automatic door or onto a lift, I think about how hard people before me fought for it.

Attendant Care: The service that makes independence possible for me and so many others. Attendants help with the daily tasks I can't do myself, getting up, dressing, showering, and getting ready for work. I call it The Great Equalizer, because it allows me to compete and live fully. I've had many attendants over the years, each one part of my story.

Community Waiver: A Community Waiver (also known as a Home and Community-Based Services Waiver or HCBS Waiver) is a Medicaid program that allows people with disabilities or older adults to receive long-term care services in their own homes or communities instead of in institutional settings like nursing homes.

CIL (Center for Independent Living): Local, community-based nonprofits run by and for people with disabilities. They teach skills, provide advocacy, and promote independent living. I came up through the CIL world, where I learned the value of community leadership and consumer control.

SILC (Statewide Independent Living Council): A state-level council that works with CILs to plan and monitor independent living services. I have been part of this network for years, helping shape how states support people with disabilities. Together, SILCs and CILs make up the backbone of the independent living movement.

Independent Living (IL) Movement: A civil rights movement led by people with disabilities demanding control over our own lives. Ed Roberts, the Father of Independent Living, mentored me. It's not just about ramps and services, it's about freedom, dignity, and self-determination. The IL Movement taught me to say, Nothing about us without us. I changed it to just "Nothing without Us" because people with disabilities are ingrained in every aspect of American life.

OVR (Office of Vocational Rehabilitation): This office changed my life. They helped pay for my college and graduate education, as well as my van modifications and early career support. OVR's investment helped me achieve financial independence. I often say I have paid back every penny in taxes and then some.

Section 504: Part of the 1973 Rehabilitation Act. The law that first made it illegal for federally funded programs to discriminate against people with disabilities. It laid the groundwork for the ADA. I was proud to witness and speak at the release of the updated 504 rules in 2024, fifty years after the original law was enacted.

Quadriplegic: Someone with paralysis in both arms and legs, usually from a spinal cord injury. I became a quadriplegic at fifteen after a football accident. It changed everything, but it didn't end anything. It was the beginning of my second life.

Spinal Cord Injury (SCI): Damage to the spinal cord that can cause partial or complete paralysis. Mine was at the C4–C5 level, meaning my injury was high on the spine. That's why I use a power wheelchair and have attendants. But like I always say, not everything on a paralyzed man is paralyzed.

501(c)(3): A tax-exempt nonprofit organization under U.S. law. NCIL, the organization I lead, is one of them. It means we don't pay federal taxes, and we exist to serve the public good, not to make a profit. It also means we must follow specific advocacy rules.

Consumer Control: A founding principle of the independent living movement. It means people with disabilities, the consumers, make the decisions about their own lives and the organizations that serve them. I live by this principle every day.

Ableism: The belief or practice that people without disabilities are somehow superior. It shows up in policies, attitudes, and systems that limit us. I have spent my life punching ableism in the face, and I plan to keep swinging. Ableism is people with disabilities' greatest challenge!

Stryker Frame: A version of a hospital bed used to rotate patients with spinal cord injuries so they don't develop pressure sores. I was placed in one after my accident at fifteen. It kept me flat on my back, staring at the ceiling for months, flipped every few hours like a pancake. It was my prison and my protector at the same time. Lying there, I had a lot of time to think about who I was going to be and who I refused to become. That Stryker Frame was where my second life began.

National Council on Independent Living (NCIL): The National Council on Independent Living is the longest-running national cross-disability, grassroots organization run by and for people with disabilities. Founded in 1982, NCIL represents thousands of organizations and individuals, including individuals with disabilities, Centers for Independent Living (CILs), Statewide Independent Living Councils (SILCs), and other organizations that advocate for the human and civil rights of people with disabilities throughout the United States. I was hired to be the executive director in 2023.

National Council on Disability (NCD): An independent federal agency advises the President, Congress, and other federal agencies on national disability policy. I was nominated by US Senator Bob Casey, Jr, and appointed by President Joe Biden in 2023.

Endorsement

You already know Mr. Braddy. You have passed him on the street, squeezed past him in line, welcomed him into your community as a symbol of your openness, and perhaps even felt that familiar, pity-warmed glow from those standing nearby. You have assumed you understood him because he appears to be an obvious book with an obvious cover. But *this* look into the Theo experience will surprise you—and ultimately give you a clearer view into yourself.

If you know Theo and his voice, you will hear his spirit unmistakably in these pages. If you do not, you will meet him here in all his authenticity, joining him as he narrates the many turns of his life's journeys. Mr. Braddy is an advocate shaped by a powerful swirl of social, cultural, personal, and deeply human circumstances. Each swirl has delivered him—sometimes gently, sometimes violently—to the platform from which the next life begins.

Memoirs of resilience and change are not new. What sets this one apart is its rare ability to invite the reader into honest self-reflection. In following Theo from a childhood bedroom whose floorboards revealed the raw earth beneath, to the Oval Office during a time of character and reverence, the reader discovers something unexpected: that these rooms are not so different after all. The constant, the connective tissue, is Mr. Braddy himself—his way of learning, questioning, listening, respecting, and contributing wherever his presence.

— Thomas J Neuville, PhD
https://www.linkedin.com/in/thomasneuville

This memoir, From Shack to White House, is a story that doesn't just flow from page to page, it flows from Theo's soul directly to the readers. Like sitting down with him, beside a warm fireplace and having a heart-to-heart conversation, one that both enlightens and challenges. Theo's tale of experiences, how they created him and, in turn, how he created others moving forward will leave the reader with no choice but to acknowledge some of life's harshest realities while simultaneously embracing some of its sweetest victories.

I know Theo personally, and from the very first sentence I could hear his voice. It leapt out from the pages, some topics familiar, some achingly foreign, but captivating throughout. His emphasis on the importance of being seen is the foundation from which he launches an amazing life and career. He shares how his voice has been refined over years and has become his greatest tool. A tool not only for himself, but for others, following in the footsteps of the giants that paved the way before him, and now becoming a giant himself.

This book is humbling, inspiring, crushing and empowering, all at the same time.

~Michael Kiel

https://www.linkedin.com/in/michael-kiel-4a4a446

Don't miss out!

Visit the website below and you can sign up to receive emails whenever Theo W. Braddy publishes a new book. There's no charge and no obligation.

https://books2read.com/r/B-A-EDJXE-LVCCI

Connecting independent readers to independent writers.

About the Author

Theo W. Braddy is a lifelong disability rights leader and the Executive Director of the National Council on Independent Living (NCIL). Appointed by President Joe Biden to the National Council on Disability, he has spent decades shaping policy and advocating for equality and justice, from his early days as a young man adjusting to life after paralysis at age 15 to becoming a national voice for people with disabilities. Theo's work has inspired and empowered thousands. He lives by the belief that every setback holds the seed of a new beginning, and every voice has the power to make change. He is married to Roe Braddy, an award-winning Author, and has two children: Kimmi Braddy and Theo Braddy, II.

Read more at RoeWrites4U.com.

About the Publisher

Roe Braddy loves her community. She is a retired educator with 32 years of teaching experience. After retiring from the classroom, she decided to take her passion and share it with her community. She is a social justice poet that writes about the injustices she sees. She is also a playwright. Roe has written and produced three live community theatre performances. Roe is also an author. She has received six literary awards for her historical romance novels. She is also published in several anthologies as well as online journals. She has also directed several theatre productions. Roe serves on several boards. (Sankofa African American Theatre Company and Nathaniel Gadsden's Writer's Workshop). Roe is the editor-in chief of the Black Wall Street PA Magazine. She has a Bachelor of Science in Special Education, a Master Degree in Education Curriculum, Design and Assessment and certifications in English and Math. Roe lives in Camp Hill, PA. She is married with two adult children.

Read more at https://www.roewrites4u.com.

www.ingramcontent.com/pod-product-compliance
Lightning Source LLC
Chambersburg PA
CBHW060528100426
42743CB00009B/1459